PAVILIONS IN PARKS

Bandstands and Rotundas Around Australia

ALISON ROSE

Photography by Belinda Brown

HALSTEAD PRESS

for Dennis

CANBERRA MMXVII
Published by Halstead Press
Gorman House, Ainslie Avenue
Braddon, Australian Capital Territory, 2612
and
Unit 66, 89 Jones Street
Ultimo, New South Wales, 2007

Designed by Kerry Klinner, megacitydesign.com. Printed in China.

National Library cataloguing-in-publication entry
Author: Alison Rose
Title: Pavilions in Parks: Bandstands and Rotundas Around Australia
ISBN: 9781925043297 (paperback)
Notes: Includes bibliography

The paper for this book has been made in a mill certified by the Forest Stewardship Council.
No old growth timber has been used in its manufacture.

contents

Introduction

I was talking to a friend about my interest in bandstands and she said she thought that they were 'dear little things'. They are, indeed, attractive structures, but they are more than just adornments in the landscape.

Chapter 1 traces the development of the building type which goes under several names. 'Bandstand', reflecting its major function, is the most common, but it is also known as rotunda, pavilion or, in earlier times, kiosk or orchestra. Examples can be found from the days of Classical Greece through the 16th century gardens of Moghul India to the modern development of platforms for band recitals in Europe in the 18th and 19th centuries. Chapter 2 brings us to Australia and the historical background of Australian bandstands. Examples follow from each state and territory, chosen for architectural, historical or social significance. Some are grand, some are simple, and each has a story to tell.

I

Small formal circular structures appeared as a building type in Classical Greece. The *tholos* in the Sanctuary of Apollo (early 4th century BC) is an example. Its function was religious, although festivals honouring the gods included music and dance. In Roman times, a building closer to the modern idea of a rotunda was the so-called Maritime Theatre in Hadrian's Villa at Tivoli outside Rome (135 AD) where Hadrian entertained his city friends.

Later, in the 7th century, a garden style called the Paradise Garden developed in Persia. Inside protective walls, a rectangular garden with avenues of trees and flower beds was divided into quarters by water channels which met at a central pond, often with a pavilion on an island in the middle.

These gardens were the inspiration for the gardens of Mughul India in the 16th and 17th centuries, the first being created on the same principles at Agra in 1526 by Babar, first Mughul emperor of North India.

Most Mughul gardens featured one or more pavilions. These delicate structures appeared in volumes of Indian scenes published in Britain in the 18th and 19th centuries, and the Indian style became popular. The Brighton Pavilion (1815–22) is a spectacular example of Indian influence, which is reflected also in 19th century bandstands and garden structures.

CLOCKWISE FROM ABOVE: A Mughul Pavilion

The Temple of Music at West Wycombe Park

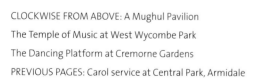
The Dancing Platform at Cremorne Gardens

PREVIOUS PAGES: Carol service at Central Park, Armidale

In England gardens of stately homes were formally laid out until the 18th century. Lancelot "Capability" Brown (1716–83) caused a revolution by designing informal gardens with sweeping vistas, often punctuated by a bridge or "temple". An example is the Temple of Music at West Wycombe Park, the home of Sir Francis Dashwood who founded the notorious Hell Fire Club. The Temple which was used for theatrical and musical performances sits on an island in a swan-shaped lake.

PLEASURE GARDENS

The development of gardens for the British public to enjoy started in 17th century London. The first of these gardens—known as 'Pleasure Gardens'—was the New Spring Gardens founded c1660 on the south bank of the Thames, near today's Vauxhall Bridge. The New Spring Gardens were simply laid out with walks and trees. In the 1730s visitors were charged entry of one shilling, a considerable amount. In 1771, the gardens were described as "a wonderful assemblage of picturesque and striking objects, pavilions, lodges, groves, grottoes, lawns, temples and cascades; porticos, colonnades and rotundas ... enlivened by mirth, freedom and good humour, and animated by an excellent band of music".

A major structure in the gardens was an elaborate three storey building with a bandstand on the first floor. Entertainment ranged from sedate tea drinking and admiring the representation of "the late fire at Hamburg, painted by Mr Marshall" to the spectacle of Madame Saqui walking a tightrope among exploding fireworks. In 1785, the name was changed to the Vauxhall Gardens. By 1805, the grand bandstand building had disappeared and by 1859 these gardens were no more.

Ranelagh Gardens were more sedate. Opened in 1742, they too had a spectacular central building for coffee, tea and concerts.

Less reputable pleasure gardens appeared in the middle of the 19th century, including the Flora Gardens in Camberwell, where in 1854 the naked Lady Godiva rode her horse, followed by an excited crowd with torches. The Montpelier Gardens exceeded this, staging a macabre cricket match between eleven one-legged pensioners and eleven one-armed pensioners with "gentlemen" betting on the result.

The Cremorne Gardens established in 1845 at Chelsea were a popular destination for Londoners. Visitors arrived by boat at Cadogan Pier and were greeted with a great many choices of entertainment. *Cruchley's London in 1865: a Handbook for Strangers, Showing where to Go, How to Get there, and what to look at* as "a place of *al fresco* amusement. Concerts, dancing, fireworks, marionettes, balloon ascents, ballets, farces and equestrian exhibitions are here provided from 3 pm until 12 pm in amazing variety."

The balloon ascents included the spectacle of Madame Poitevin's ride skywards as Europa sitting on a startled white heifer! People complained and the proprietor was fined for cruelty to animals.

The 12 acre (5 hectare) park had avenues for evening strolls and many arbours for quiet courtship, but it was dominated by a large central pavilion lit by hundreds of lamps. A fifty piece orchestra was surrounded by a dancing platform.

By 1877, the citizens of Chelsea had become fed up with the influx of rowdy visitors and after several changes of lessee Cremorne Gardens closed. One former lessee was James Ellis, who emigrated after being declared bankrupt, and started a similar Cremorne Gardens in Melbourne in 1853.

BANDSTANDS IN PUBLIC PARKS

Parallel to the development of structures for music and dancing in pleasure gardens was the rise of bandstands for entertainment in public places such as parks and seaside esplanades.

A bandstand in the park had a useful social purpose. It brought music to many people who would have no other opportunity to hear it, it was a way to meet old friends and for the young to find new friends.

Other uses developed—bandstands became platforms for speech making, saluting bases for military parades, places for farewells and welcoming home troops, and meeting places—"I will meet you at the bandstand."

Some bandstands were built specially to commemorate important events: Queen Victoria's Diamond Jubilee and the accession of King Edward VII were popular.

BANDSTAND DESIGNS

The idea of the bandstand in the park appealed to Victorians and bandstands blossomed in parks all over Great Britain. Their design arose from practical considerations—elevated so people could see the musicians, with a roof to keep the bandsmen and instruments dry and to improve the acoustics. Most were octagonal, usually seven to eight metres across, and access was gained via a set of steps—although at least two later Australian examples did away with the steps, bandsmen emerging instead from the basement through a trapdoor in the floor.

Two early bandstands, built in the Royal Horticultural Society's Garden at Kensington in London in 1861, were designed by Captain Francis Fowkes, an army engineer. With cast iron columns and timber rooves covered in a zinc sheeting, they were described by *The Illustrated London News* as "an elegant structure with a roof of

Oriental character". Books including illustrations of Indian architecture were popular in Victorian times and Captain Fowkes' designs reflect this interest. This exciting new development, combining the structural and decorative elements of cast iron, soon spread around the world.

The catalyst for this blooming was the culmination of advances in techniques for the casting of iron. Founders (to be distinguished from smiths, who worked with wrought iron) originally only worked brass and copper, but by 1532 the craft of cast iron founding was well enough established in Great Britain for the founders to build themselves a Hall for the Worshipful Company of Founders in London.

It was difficult to get a high enough temperature for casting iron from the charcoal then available, but in 1713, Abraham Derby at Coalbrookdale discovered a method of using coke which gave a much higher firing temperature. This advance in technique revolutionised the craft. Accurate moulds now could be made in a sand casting bed and identical castings made to that pattern.

Cast iron was first made for machinery parts, but later was widely used for fences and balcony railings, replacing the much more labour intensive working of wrought iron. Cast iron is fragile in tension, but strong in compression, making it ideal for cast columns. The invention of gas street lighting led to a plethora of cast iron street lamp designs, from the basic to the extravagant.

These lamp posts, fences, railings and many other cast iron designs, including bandstand columns and decorations, were illustrated in splendid pattern books published by Scottish foundries. These foundries were clustered around Glasgow where coal, ironstone and water were all plentiful.

Probably the most widely known and influential Scottish foundry was Walter Macfarlane and Company's vast Saracen Foundry which by 1872 employed 1,400 metalworkers. Macfarlane's catalogues with their elegant illustrations were sent around the world to such places as India, South Africa, Bermuda, and Australia, and their designs were much copied.

There are only two known fully imported cast iron bandstands in Australia, both manufactured by Macfarlane and Co. They are in Elder Park, Adelaide and Queen's Gardens, Maryborough, Queensland.

The late E. Graeme Robertson in his comprehensive 1977 book, *Cast Iron Decoration—a World Survey*, shows the extent to which cast iron was used. Nowhere was it more enthusiastically embraced than in Australia which, according to Robertson, probably has more surviving cast iron than anywhere else.

ABOVE: The Royal Horticultural Society's Bandstand, Kensington
RIGHT: Miners' Aggregate Meeting, Lambton, Newcastle

II

Australian society underwent enormous change in the middle of the 19th century. It started with the discovery of gold. The first gold rush began after Edward Hargraves in 1851 looked into his pan of gravel from the Lewis Ponds, a tributary of the Macquarie River in New South Wales, and saw the specks of gold. "There it is," he said. "This is a memorable day in the history of New South Wales. I shall be made a baronet ... and my old horse will be stuffed, and put into a glass-case and sent to the British Museum." Neither of those prophesies eventuated, but the gold rushes that ensued changed the character of Australia forever.

Before the discovery of gold, the eastern Australian colonies were heavily dependent on convict labour. Although there had been agitation to end transportation, it was not until gold was discovered that the British government finally agreed that the system was breaking down and there was no point in sending convicts to the colonies when everyone, including ticket-of-leave men, was downing tools and heading for the diggings. Charles FitzRoy, Governor of New South Wales, remarked at the time: "Few English criminals ... would not regard a free passage to the goldfields via Hobart Town as a great boon."

The social change was fundamental. Gold was the great leveller—it did not matter about your background or your level of education. "We be the aristocracy now, and the aristocracy now be we" sang miners drinking in Melbourne's grog shops. The immigration of gold seekers and the subsequent wealth that flowed from the goldfields to the towns caused a population explosion. Melbourne benefitted most from this river of gold. The population grew from 139,000 in 1861 to 490,000 in 1891 and this led to a building boom just when cast iron decoration was becoming popular. Initially, the iron castings were all imported, but local foundries were quickly established to make copies with imported pig iron. Gradually local designs with Australian flora and fauna motifs were developed.

From terrace houses to public buildings, cast iron balcony railings, friezes, end brackets, lace topped towers and delicate finials proliferated.

Country towns also benefitted from the gold which abounded in the surrounding countryside. Most settlements of any size in Victoria, where the most gold was found, were proclaimed as towns between 1850 and 1860 and as one writer commented in Cassell's *Picturesque Australasia*, published in 1889: "All seemed to be laid out in the same fashion, planted with the same trees and have the same State school, town hall and post office."

Their wide streets width can be attributed to the foresight of the first Chief Surveyor of Victoria. William Dawson used a "3-chain width" (20 metres) for the main streets of country towns. This generous street layout was adopted in new country towns in all colonies, providing room in the centre of the carriageway for gardens, memorials—and bandstands. The other popular location for the town bandstand was the park where the bandstand, and often its attendant cast iron fountain, provided a focal point.

The self confidence of late Victorian Australia led to a desire for self education. Every city had to have a museum and a botanical garden and every town, whatever its size, aspired to a School of Arts or Mechanics Institute and a municipal band. Of course, a band needed a bandstand and so we have the concept and design imported intact from "the Old Country". Municipal bands flourished in the late 19th and early 20th centuries. They were usually formed by a group of enthusiastic citizens, the local council, or, in mining towns, the mining company. The band played at all ceremonial occasions, which often were centred on the bandstand.

As in England, bandstands were also built to commemorate special events, and as war memorials.

The concert in the town bandstand was often the only opportunity for people to hear live music as well as to socialise. The music and the band were not always appreciated. Banjo Paterson in his poem "In Defence of the Bush" declaimed:

Do you hear the silver chiming of the bell-bird on the range?
But, perchance, the wild birds' music by your senses was despised,

For you say you'll stay in townships till the bush is civilised.
Would you make it a tea-garden, and on Sundays have a band
Where the "blokes" may take their "donahs" with a "public" close at hand:
You had better stick to Sydney and make merry with the "push",
For the bush will never suit you, and you'll never suit the bush.

Mining towns benefitted from the influx of British immigrants who brought with them the tradition of the "works band". Bands were also formed by such bodies as the railways and tramways. A rotunda was built at each terminus of three tram lines in Adelaide in 1909 and on special occasions the Adelaide Tramways Band Club would board a specially converted tram and play all the way to the rotunda. The concerts at Henley Beach terminus rotunda attracted thousands and the "band tram" had to make many trips.

Bandstands were also used as places to conduct public meetings. The illustration shows miners gathering for a "miners' aggregate" meeting at the bandstand in Lambton, Newcastle in 1896.

Banding declined in the 1930s with the advent of jazz bands, radio and improvements in recording, but it never entirely disappeared. Today, there is a revival of band music with concert bands and traditional brass bands. Anzac Day marches, for example, demonstrate that bands not only continue to be part of public life, but that in recent years many new, non-military bands have made an appearance.

PLEASURE GARDENS

The pleasure garden was another form of popular entertainment imported from England. By 1853, James Ellis, formerly a proprietor of London's Cremorne Gardens in Chelsea, had moved to Melbourne and was advertising his Cremorne Pleasure Gardens on the Yarra River. Visitors came up the river by boat and could take their pick of such attractions as "fireworks, pavilions, grottoes, sideshows, spectacles, and concerts". A central feature was a large bandstand surrounded by a dance floor. Among the spectacles offered was a reproduction of the siege of Sebastopol with fireworks made more realistic by the gunfire of the 40th Regiment.

The garden, like its English progenitor, gradually became noisier and gained a disreputable reputation. It finally closed in 1864.

Melburnians in search of relaxation and some excitement could also travel by ferry to the Bayside towns of Queenscliff and Sorrento, with their bandstands to entertain the "trippers".

Sydney's Cremorne Gardens followed much the same course as Melbourne's.

TOP LEFT: Sketch of gold prospectors, by S.T. Gill
ABOVE: Cast iron designs with Australian motifs
LEFT: Fountain in Victoria Park, Forbes, New South Wales
PREVIOUS PAGES: The Federation bandstand at Ipswich, Queensland, built 1913

TOP LEFT: SS Titanic Memorial Bandstand at Ballarat, Victoria

LEFT: Plaques on the rotunda in Cook Park, Orange, New South Wales

ABOVE: Poster for Cremorne Gardens, Sydney

OPPOSITE PAGE: The bandstand at Clare, South Australia being restored, 2012

Opened on Robertson's Point on the north shore of Sydney Harbour in 1856 by Joseph Simmonds, an actor, auctioneer and storekeeper, the gardens advertised jugglers, tightrope walkers and circus performers, archery, gymnastics and "refreshments at Sydney prices".

A dance floor and pavilion were built and "a high standard of dancing was expected". Evening masked balls cost 7 shillings 6 pence for gentlemen and 5 shillings for ladies. Together with the round trip ferry fare and entrance fee of 2 shilings it made for an expensive evening. There were complaints about the lack of lighting and the poor food. Soon the arrival of "undesirable elements" caused a rapid deterioration and the gardens closed in 1862. Despite surviving only six years, the gardens gave the name Cremorne Point to the former Robertson's Point and the suburb spreading northward from the point was named Cremorne.

A more successful Sydney pleasure garden was Correy's Pleasure Garden at Cabarita Point on the Parramatta River, a popular destination for Sydneysiders from the 1880s to 1918. Thomas Correy and his family planted trees and gardens, laid out a cricket pitch, a running track and a children's playground, and provided summerhouses for picnic parties. In 1887, a dance pavilion with a specially constructed tallowwood floor, holding up to 900 dancers and a ten piece orchestra, was built. To get them into the mood, visitors on ferries to the grounds were often entertained by an onboard band.

The growing popularity of the motor car spelt the end of the attractions of Correy's Pleasure Garden and it closed in 1918. The tallowwood dance floor found a new home in another bandstand in Port Pirie, South Australia.

FEDERATION—A NEW COUNTRY AND A NEW STYLE OF ARCHITECTURE

The 1880s were boom times in Australia. Minerals were discovered—tin in Tasmania and silver and lead at Broken Hill, for example—and speculation in mining, land and building was rife, much of it funded by borrowings from London. As after boom times everywhere, the bubble eventually burst and the colonies slid into recession. Bank closures began in 1890 and by 1893 the recession had deepened into depression. Other causes were the severe drought which in places had started as far back as 1880, the series of strikes by maritime workers and Broken Hill miners in 1890, and the 1891 Queensland shearers' strike.

Meanwhile, the movement towards Federation was gaining strength. The first Federation Conference was held in February 1890 when thirteen colonial delegates agreed to establish a convention which would consider a federal constitution under

the British Crown. In March 1891, the delegates debated a draft constitution, but no further work was done while the Depression lasted. The Convention reconvened in 1897 and by July 1900 all the colonies had agreed to federate. The bill for an Australian constitution passed through the British Parliament on 21 May 1900 and on Federation Day, 1 January 1901, Lord Hopetoun was sworn in as Governor General in a rotunda in Sydney's Centennial Park.

Federation was a watershed in Australian history—there was confidence in a new country and there was a unique style of architecture to match—the "Federation style". This developed from several overseas influences, the major one being the English so-called 'Queen Anne' style, which had little other than the use of red face brick to do with the Queen Anne period. Several architects designing in this style had immigrated from Britain and their modern designs were enthusiastically embraced. The red brick, newly available Marseilles roof tiles, and the Arts and Crafts movement's timber detail appealed to the citizens of the new country. The design was modified to suit Australian climates with verandas and balconies, and became known as the Federation style.

The design of bandstands followed suit—cast iron columns and cast iron lace were out and in were timber columns, timber brackets and decorative timber fretwork.

Many bandstands were built during this time of national confidence and it was not until the period between the two World Wars that bandstand building almost came to a halt.

During the Great Depression of the 1930s, a unique variation of the bandstand was built in 1934 in the Dr. H.J. Foley Memorial Rest Park in Glebe, a suburb of Sydney. Donated by Mr Grace, the owner of a large department store, the Wireless House, a modest brick structure, housed a radio speaker with amplifiers which broadcast news and music from 10 am to 10 pm. It has recently been restored.

After the Second World War, concrete 'sound shells' became popular for outdoor musical concerts. Some were well designed, but others were extremely ugly. You can see the crumbling remains in some small towns. Interest in the restoration of old bandstands grew in the 1980s and saved many attractive examples from oblivion.

Today, there is interest in bandstands for their practical uses as well as their decorative function and towns and suburbs are building new bandstands. Some are in Federation style; others provide a more contemporary home for today's musical events, as can be seen in following chapters. ❖

ABOVE LEFT: The Glebe Wireless House
ABOVE RIGHT: Arriving by ferry at Correy's Pleasure Garden

THE PAVILIONS

new farm park
brisbane

Like New South Wales and Tasmania, Queensland began as a penal colony. Governor Brisbane sent an exploratory party under John Oxley north from Sydney in 1823 to look at Moreton Bay—noted but not explored by Captain Cook fifty years earlier. Far away from any other settlement, it was an ideal location for a penal settlement.

In September 1824, Lieutenant Henry Miller sailed to Moreton Bay with fifty settlers, thirty of whom were volunteer prisoners hoping to win an early ticket of leave. They landed at Redcliffe, also known as Humpy Bong, and, after trying to farm the poor soil there, moved the settlement to the present site of Brisbane. The colony under Captain Peter Bishop struggled on in its new location and when he left in March 1826 could boast of only a few poor buildings—not even a gaol—and a few hectares of wheat, potatoes and pumpkins, some grown at the "new farm" on a bend in the river.

Bishop's successor, the dreaded Commander Logan, promptly built the gaol into which he put as many convicts as possible. His regime of brutality came to a suitably violent end in October 1830 when he was killed by a group of Aborigines whom he had also terrorised.

By 1831, the convict population had grown to 1,020, but thereafter Moreton Bay penal settlement slowly declined and in 1840 all remaining convicts were sent to Sydney. After military rule ceased in Brisbane in 1842 all farmland was farmed by

free settlers. By 1843, the area of the "new farm" had been divided into "suburban allotments"—large enough to be used as small farms. Richard Jones, later the first Brisbane member of the New South Wales Parliament, bought 37 hectares (91 acres) of allotments in 1847 and called his property New Farm. It later included a race course, which was moved to Eagle Farm in 1861. Industry developed along the waterfront in following decades, most prominently the CSR Sugar Refinery in 1893.

In 1884, Nehemiah Bartley wrote a letter to the newspaper suggesting that the growing population of the New Farm area needed some open space—eventually, in 1913, about 15 hectares (37 acres) were sold to the city of Brisbane for a park.

Designed by the first Brisbane City Parks Superintendant, Henry Moore, the planting of the new park began in 1914. Some of his original layout survives, the most impressive feature being the magnificent avenue of jacarandas. Modifications have been made over the years to reflect the park's changing use. A major redesign by Harry Oakman in the 1940s introduced the extensive rose beds that are so much admired today.

Placed in an ideal position close to the Brisbane River, the bandstand and kiosk were designed by Albert Henry Foster who became City Architect in 1913. The Federation-style timber framed bandstand survives, featuring musical motifs, paired timber columns, timber balustrades and gables over the frieze above the two entrances, but the kiosk burnt down in 2000. The bandstand (which has a twin in Gympie) is very popular for weddings and the seats are a cool resting placed from the summer sun.

maryborough
queensland

Maryborough, 250 kilometres north of Brisbane, is home to one of only two fully imported rotundas in Australia. It stands in Queen's Park on the banks of the Mary River.

The region was first surveyed in 1842 and in 1847 settlers began to arrive, settling by the Mary River, named by Governor Fitzroy after his wife. The river became the route for the export of timber and wool from the surrounding areas. Wharves and a wool store were built upstream from the present town, but frequent flooding caused the port to move to its present location. The port closed in 1974, but some remains of wharves can be seen still on the foreshore walkway.

In 1859, Maryborough was gazetted an official port of entry and between 1859 and 1901 more than 22,000 migrants, mostly from England, Germany and Scandinavia came to Hervey Bay on immigrant ships and were ferried upriver to Maryborough in smaller boats. Later that century, Kanaka labourers from the Pacific Islands were brought to work in the canefields.

The discovery of gold in 1867 at Gympie, 90 kilometres to the south, stimulated industry in Maryborough. Timber mills provided timber for pit props in the goldmines and engineering works were established in 1869 to make machinery for the mines at Gympie and, later, other Queensland mines.

The engineering company, Walker Bros., made machinery for sugar mills as the sugar industry became established. The firm branched out into shipbuilding, completing thirteen vessels in the 1870s and 80s. Two more ships were built after 1917. Then shipbuilding ceased until the shipyard was reactivated in 1939 when seven mine sweepers and three frigates were ordered. The first completed was the minesweeper HMAS *Cairns*, launched on 7 October 1941. The only surviving World War II Walker Bros. ship is the River class frigate HMAS *Diamantina*, now permanently at home in dry dock at the Queensland Maritime Museum in Brisbane. The shipyard closed in 1974 and the remaining buildings were demolished in 2008. A memorial with the names of all the ships built for the Royal Australian Navy was erected on the riverfront walkway and dedicated in 1993.

Queen's Park was first vested as a "botanical gardens reserve" in 1866 and became a botanical garden in 1873. Many of the pre-1900 trees survive. Queens Park is heritage listed as are the sandstone entrance gates and the stirring War Memorial just outside. Designed by P.O.E. Hawkes, the memorial portrays a marble statue of Nike, the goddess of victory, standing on top of an obelisk with sculptures of a sailor, a soldier, an airman and a Red Cross nurse at its base.

The rotunda in the park was commissioned by Janet Melville in memory of her brother, Andrew Melville, who had been Mayor of Maryborough in 1863. Miss Melville asked the local MP, Andrew Heron-Wilson, to choose a suitable rotunda when he went to the Glasgow Exhibition in 1888.

This he did and the Macfarlane and Co. rotunda that duly arrived from Scotland on 31 December 1889 was erected in March the next year. The rotunda originally housed an ornate fountain, known colloquially as the Fairy Fountain, even though it is decorated with herons. The fountain now sits close by in the garden, having been moved out in 1905 to convert the rotunda into a bandstand. The bandstand among its handsome trees is still a popular gathering place and the town band plays there on the last Sunday of the month. ❖

Bandstands and rotundas are not found only in cities and
large country towns. Smaller communities, too, have a
sense of civic pride and have developed parks and founded
municipal bands. Here are two of them.

toogoolawah

McConnel Park, established c1906 remains the centre of the community in Toogoolawah. The park encompasses a tennis court, cricket pitch, guide hut and scout den, the War Memorial built c1916 and the bandstand. A church and hall stand adjacent.

The land for the park was donated by James Henry McConnel whose father was the first European to settle in the Brisbane Valley, taking up the Cresswick Run in 1841. The McConnels were very much involved in the life of the town which grew up to service their condensed milk factory, established in 1898, and the growing number of farms in the valley. The McConnels employed a contractor to build houses for their farmers, donated the land for the church and park, and supported local organisations.

The church was designed by Queensland architect Robin Dod, one of a small group of architects at the end of the 19th century, who designed buildings suitable for Queensland. His work featured wide verandas and strong, simple timber detailing. As Neville Lund said in Architects of Australia, "his specific contribution was the development of appropriate architecture for the sub-tropical climate". This can be seen clearly in the design of the church.

A brass band was founded in Toogoolawah in 1919 and the bandstand, believed to have been donated by the McConnel family, was built in 1925 to accommodate it. It is uncertain whether Dod's office designed the bandstand, but its timber detail certainly reflects his style. The bandstand today remains a focal point of a well cared for and well used place of recreation for the people of Toogoolawah. ❖

ERECTED
BY THE
RESIDENTS OF APPLE TREE CREEK.
IN RECOGNITION OF THOSE WHO
ENLISTED FROM APPLE TREE CREEK.
AND MADE THE SUPREME SACRIFICE
IN THE GREAT WAR
1914 - 1919

"THEIR NAME LIVETH FOR EVERMORE."

BLATCHFORD. G. T.
BROUGHAM. W.
HALL. E.
HARLEY. J.
HOWARD. P. A.
KLING. C.
KERR. J.
NEWBIGGING. G.
NEWBIGGING. W.
O'CALLAGHAN. G.
PAGE. P. W.
PITT. J. O.
TAYLOR. A.
TAYLOR. W. H
TREVOR. A

apple tree creek

Apple Tree Creek (known as Bodalla until 1962) is a popular and welcoming stopping place on the Bruce Highway between Childers and Gin Gin in Queensland. The area was first opened up for farming in the 1870s. The Isis Central Sugar Mill established in 1895 is still in operation, giving a boost to the local economy. The school was opened in 1896 and in the first years of the 20th century the Recreation Ground was developed with a sports oval and bandstand, built in 1911 for the Apple Tree Creek Citizens Brass Band, which used it for many years.

A heritage-listed war memorial, designed by A.L. Petrie and entirely subscribed for locally, was unveiled on 21 March 1921.

By the 1970s, the bandstand was derelict. It was saved by the local community and extensive repairs were made in 1973. It is one of the few buildings remaining from Apple Tree Creek's early days, a symbol of the pride taken in its history by this small country town. ❖

the strand
townsville

One of Australia's most delicate and delightful bandstands is in the Strand, the waterfront park of Townsville, Queensland's second largest city. The Strand extends 2.2 kilometres along Townsville's foreshore, separating the city from the sea.

Founded in 1864 as a port for the processing and export of beef carcasses from the hinterland, the town was first named Castleton after the dramatic red granite hill which rises behind it. The town's name was changed in 1865 after its founder, Robert Towns, and the settlement grew rapidly with the establishment of sugar and cotton plantations and the construction of the railway line to Charters Towers in 1882. Nearly all of Charters Towers' enormous gold output was shipped through Townsville. Exports of meat and sugar maintained Townsville's prosperity after the gold at Charters Towers and nearby Ravensworth had run out.

During the Second World War, Townsville became one of the most important military bases in the South Pacific and was at one stage the headquarters of General Douglas Macarthur, Allied Supreme Commander South West Pacific. Macarthur occupied the Customs House on the Strand, and the adjacent Queens Hotel was used as an officers' club. Gun emplacements were built along the waterfront to defend the city which was bombed three times.

The earliest development on the Strand was the Council Baths built in 1890. Women were admitted to the baths only on Tuesdays and Fridays. In 1910, mayor and alderman John Henry Tyack began raising funds for a bandstand to be built on the Strand opposite the Queens Hotel which he owned. The bandstand was designed gratis by Arthur Polin, the Queensland Manager of a Sydney firm of architects, Eaton, Bates, Polin, who had also designed Tyack's grand Queens Hotel.

The area of the Strand between King and Cleveland Streets was declared "a reserve for park purposes" in 1912 at Tyack's instigation. Unfortunately he died before the bandstand was completed. It was dedicated to his memory at its opening on 27 September 1913.

The bandstand was immediately popular. It was also used at night and in November 1914 the Townsville Coal and Coke Company offered to maintain "the five high power burners in the Band Rotunda for five shillings for each month". In September 1926, Council decided to charge 10 shillings and sixpence per evening for the use of the band rotunda except for "bands, musical entertainments and Council functions".

Another development on the Strand was the Seaview Baths at its southern end, opened in 1921. A dance pavilion was added in 1931, extending over the water on timber piles. A band played for the dancers and the music was played over loudspeakers for the swimmers, too.

The park was renamed ANZAC Memorial Park in 1934 and a memorial arch was built over the entrance gate.

The bandstand was moved to its present location in 1960 to make way for the Centenary Fountain. Major redevelopments were made in 1999 after destructive monsoonal storms in 1997 and 1998. Three headlands were formed to protect the beaches and sea walls and new walkways and play areas were built to make the Strand a very attractive place, with the bandstand retaining its elegant presence.

Opening of bandstand on the Strand.

lissner park
charters towers

With its own Stock Exchange and many substantial buildings which still survive, Charters Towers was once Australia's richest town. The source of this wealth was gold; first alluvial gold and then rich reef gold.

Three prospectors, Hugh Mosman, George Clarke and James Fraser, with their Aboriginal servant, Jupiter, were prospecting in the area in 1871 when Jupiter found alluvial gold at the base of Tower Hill. The sample was taken to nearby Ravenswood and the location of the find was named Charters Towers after W.S. Charters, the mining warden at Ravenswood.

Most of the alluvial gold was exhausted by the mid-1870s, but great prosperity came with the start of reef mining. Unlike the batteries which crushed the ore at other goldfields, the giant Venus Battery at Charters Towers could be used by all. It can still be visited.

Because the gold was discovered after the southern goldfields were mostly played out, Charters Towers was able to develop in an orderly fashion. Experienced miners came from the south followed by businessmen who would "grub stake" miners—back them financially in return for a share of their finds. The town prospered and such was the confidence of the residents that the editor of the local newspaper called Charters Towers "the World" and said that "everything any civilised person could want" could be found there.

The Mining Exchange formed by a group of miners in 1885 gave local people a chance to invest in their booming town. The Stock Exchange in the splendid Royal Arcade opened in 1890. Buyers and sellers negotiated with brokers until the "call", when for a short time deals were done. The exchange was so successful that there were three calls a day at its peak. English investors poured money into the town, stimulated, no doubt, by the entrepreneurial Tom Mills who was owner or part owner of a great deal of Charters Towers. He organised daily stamping of Charters Towers ore at the gold mining exhibit in the Queen's Court at the Colonial and Indian Exposition in London in 1886.

In 1897, the editor of *The North Queensland Mining Register* had this to say:

All in 25 years. The well wooded and comparatively flat basin surrounding the small ridges below the Gap through which the pioneers came has long been denuded of its trees. Streets of fine shops and residences have sprung up, cold air stores, telephones, electric light, gas light, electric fans and other adjuncts of up-to-date civilisation are employed and 20,000 souls now sleep nightly within a radius of four miles of the spot where the prospectors pitched their camp a little over 25 years ago.

The mention of cold air stores and electric fans shows that the citizens of Charters Towers were managing to deal with their extreme climate.

The euphoria was shortlived. Gold production peaked in 1899 and then declined rapidly. Charters Towers then became a quiet centre for surrounding pastoral districts. An advantage of this change in fortunes is that most of the town's Victorian buildings remain intact. In the Second World War, four airfields were built as back up for the military installations in Townsville and an American bomber squadron was relocated to Charters Towers after the fall of the Philippines.

Lissner Park, seven hectares in the middle of the town, was gazetted as a recreation reserve in 1883. By 1891, *The Miner* could report that "the reserve was well fenced and planted with shade trees which are beginning to look really well". The trees are still looking really well and provide much needed shade.

The splendid Boer War Memorial Kiosk in the park was also designed to keep the sun off the citizens. A Patriotic Fund for soldiers and their families affected by the Boer War had £12,000 left over after the war and the Municipal Council suggested it could be used to build a kiosk to commemorate the eighty-two volunteers from the district's Kennedy Regiment who enlisted between 1899 and 1901, joining the other Queensland contingents for South Africa. A prize offered for the best design was won by Mr F. Jorgensen from the Technical College. The builder's name is not known, but the decorative cast iron work was supplied by local foundry of Walton and Millgate. The Boer War Memorial Kiosk was built in 1910 and the names of all the

district's volunteers are listed on a panel inside.

The Kiosk was to be "opened every day from 10am to 10pm selling refreshments and boiling water at a penny a gallon". Over 7,000 citizens went to the ceremony of which the mayor, S. H. Thorpe opened the kiosk, which was followed by a "promenade concert". Celebrations went on until night with the Kiosk, band rotunda (since demolished) and fountain "brightly lit".

Part of the park was nearly lost in 1918 when Tom Mills came back to Charters Towers with a scheme to reopen his Day Dawn mine following the lode that ran under the park. This required putting down a shaft in the park "but avoiding the Kiosk". A public meeting voted for the idea, but fortunately it never eventuated and Tom Mills went back to England and occupied himself writing a book on *The Detection of German U-Boats by the Use of Trained Sea Gulls*.   ❖

parramatta
sydney

Soon after settlement, the infant colony at Sydney Cove was running out of land suitable for farming. Thin layers of soil on sandstone and an unreliable water supply from the Tank Stream prompted Governor Phillip and a party of men to row up the Parramatta River to the limits of navigation. There they found an abundance of good agricultural land suitable for a settlement and named the area Rose Hill after George Rose, one of the Secretaries to the Treasury in London, a patron of Phillip's.

The next day, one of the party, Surgeon-General White, described their landing place: "The trees around us were immensely large, and the tops of them were filled with loraquets and paraquets of exquisite beauty, which chattered to such a degree that we could scarcely hear each other speak". The "loraquets" became known as "Rose Hillers" which later became rosellas. On 2 November, Governor Phillip returned to Rose Hill with Surveyor-General Augustus Alt to lay out the roads of the new town.

In November 1790, the indefatigable Watkin Tench, a captain of marines, went to Rose Hill and described how the main street leading from the landing place to the new, very modest Government House would "make Pall Mall and Portland Place hide their heads in shame" (p.155). He also made a thorough inspection of the crops which had been planted and spent some time talking to James Ruse, the first genuine farmer in Australia. Ruse, who had been a farmer in Cornwall, was an emancipist, a convict who had served his term, but did not want to return to England. Phillip offered to let the emancipists farm land, lending them tools while they still drew their rations from the Government Store. Ruse managed to get himself "off the store" by February 1791 and was rewarded by Phillip with 30 acres (12 hectares) of freehold land, the first in Australia.

On 2 June 1791, the name of the settlement was changed to Parramatta, meaning in the local Aboriginal language "the place where eels jump up", referring to the rapids at the navigable limits of the river. The river was the main means of travel between Sydney Town and Parramatta for many years.

The first ferry, named the Rose Hill Packet, more familiarly known as "The Lump", carried passengers, mail and some cargo up and down the river. The rough foot track from Sydney was cleared for wheeled traffic in 1789 and Parramatta became a rural centre as farming land was developed. Two early farm houses still standing are Elizabeth Farm, named after the wife of John Macarthur, and Experiment Farm cottage.

Governor Macquarie laid out new streets in 1811 and oversaw the construction of many substantial buildings, including the Lancer Barracks in 1820 (still occupied by the Australian Army) and additions to Government House.

Industries started in the early 1800s—a brick kiln, flour mill and a brewery supplied the wants of the residents of Parramatta. The surrounding farms supplied the food for the growing town, as well as for Sydney. The railway from Sydney opened in 1855, giving an enormous boost to industry and commerce and bringing an influx of people. In 1871, the population numbered 6,000; by 1891, it had nearly doubled to 11,500.

Parramatta's first gaol was built by Governor Hunter in 1797 on the north side of the river. When it was demolished in 1842, after being replaced by a new gaol, the land was called Gaol Green until it was given to the people of Parramatta and named Prince Alfred Square.

By January 1890, councillors were considering "beautifying" Prince Alfred Square which was described as an "eyesore". An amount of £600 was approved in April 1890 and the Mayor, W.J. Ferris, announced that he had had plans prepared for a bandstand in the park. This did not go down well with some aldermen who complained that they had not given approval, to which Mayor Ferris grandly replied that it did not matter, as the funds had already been approved. Despite a good deal of council bickering, the bandstand was built, the official opening taking place on 12 January 1891. The bandstand is a good example of Victorian design with delicate ironwork and slender cast iron columns—an attractive addition to a Victorian park. I have not been able to find information about the designer or builder.

Industry was stimulated during the First World War and many ex-servicemen moved to Parramatta after the war. Horses and carts gave way to motor cars and the radio and the movies changed people's sources of entertainment. The splendid Roxy Cinema, opened in 1930, is still in business. The town suffered through the Great Depression along with the rest of Australia, but the advent of the Second World War once again gave a boost to Parramatta, which had been proclaimed a city in 1938. Since then, the city has become the centre for the western half of Sydney with a major hospital and the University of Western Sydney, and a centre for government and commerce.

You can still take a ferry up the river to Parramatta and walk up Watkin Tench's grand street to Old Government House. Scattered among the high rise buildings are elegant Georgian buildings, reminders of the days when Parramatta was the most important settlement after Sydney. ❖

lane cove
sydney

What is now the Sydney Municipality of Lane Cove was for thousands of years the home of the Cam-mer-ray-gal people. Leaving only rock carvings and shell middens as evidence of their long history, they were driven away after white settlers arrived in 1788.

Lieutenant Ralph Clark landed near the entrance of the Lane Cove River on 14 February 1790 and the first land grants were made in 1794. At first not many were taken up; the land was hilly and bush covered, so it was mostly utilised for timber getting, which was of major importance for the infant colony.

The area was also a useful hiding place for absconding convicts and other questionable characters, including the notorious Tambourine Nell who thought it wise to move her "house of ill repute" to what later became known as Tambourine Bay on the Lane Cove River.

During the 19th century, the name Lane Cove was used for a much larger area of the north shore which became the Borough of North Willoughby in 1865. Lane Cove finally became a municipality in February 1895 and slowly developed into a thriving suburb with both tram and ferry services to the city. Lane Cove's shopping centre developed at the T-junction of Burns Bay Road (running East–West) and Longueville Road (running North–South).

Traffic built up over the years; by the 1960s, the Lane Cove Chamber of Commerce, concerned about the noise and dust and lack of parking, organised a survey of local people's concerns about the shopping centre. As a result, on 29 February 1969, the Chamber of Commerce recommended three levels of parking in an adjacent street; a pedestrian mall at ground level; and the diversion of heavy traffic around the shopping centre.

Lane Cove Council agreed something had to be done, and on 18 February approached the School of Architecture at the University of New South Wales with the suggestion that the redevelopment of the shopping centre be a senior student project. The students' schemes were exhibited in February 1971, attracting lots of local people.

The Council formed a Special Committee on Lane Cove Development and by July consultants were asked for ideas on the improvement of the shopping centre. The successful proposal by Plant Location International included closing the last block of Burns Bay Road to form what the feasibility study called a plaza "with outdoor restaurants and stalls providing a lively village atmosphere".

In February 1974, the Council commissioned landscape architect Harry Howard, who worked for years on a design for closure of the road and the proposed plaza. Police

Lloyd Rees
1895 – 1988

"A CITY IS THE GREATEST
WORK OF ART POSSIBLE"

SCULPTOR LAWRENCE BECK 1983

permission to close the road for ninety days was given in September 1974. When the Town Clerk asked for opinions, he was deluged with comments: "against" were the affected shopkeepers and "for" were those, mostly women, who appreciated having places to sit and the opportunity to move around the shops without dodging traffic.

The subsequent battle between opponents and supporters raged for months. The Council eventually voted for permanent closure of the last block of Burns Bay Road on 10 March 1975. That Christmas, Carols by Candlelight were held in the plaza and the first dedicated pedestrian plaza in New South Wales became reality. It is today universally appreciated and recognised for the convenient, safe and pleasant shopping and public activities space it provides—a tribute to the foresight of the Council, the Chamber of Commerce and citizens of the time.

The Plaza, officially opened in November 1977, became an immediate success— "the new heart of Lane Cove" commentators wrote. In 1980 the well known artist and local resident Lloyd Rees wrote to the Council suggesting the plaza needed "a visual focus ... such as a bandstand with a touch of phantasy about it; but which would be very useful for summer shade and for public addresses and music etc". He offered to donate $5,000 towards it, and Harry Howard (whom Rees had at Sydney University School of Architecture) was commissioned by the Council to design options in consultation with Lloyd Rees. It was eventually decided the bandstand would be made from a translucent membrane suspended from eight arched stainless steel pipe frames—an elegant and practical design answering Lloyd Rees's wish for a "touch of phantasy".

The Lane Cove Plaza bandstand which was opened by Lloyd Rees on 9 April 1983 has been immensely popular, giving the suburb a lively focus. There is always something going on there and the bandstand is used almost every weekend, fulfilling Lloyd Rees's vision in every way.

gulgong
new south wales

"Unique" is a word freely used to describe special places, but Gulgong in the Central West of New South Wales really is unique. It is probably the best preserved mining town in Australia owing to a unique set of circumstances: its location in rich farming country meant that miners could become farmers when the gold ran out, and the town's shopkeepers and merchants could stay in business. Its place in literature in the poetry of Henry Lawson and in the stories about diggers and bushrangers by Rolf Boldrewood; the photography of the "roaring days" of the 1870s by Merlin and Bayliss; and visits from travellers such as Anthony Trollope who described life in Gulgong in 1871 helped keep Gulgong in the public eye.

The Wiradjuri people who had lived here for thousands of years saw their first Europeans in 1822 when George and Henry Cox established their property "Guntawang" near the future Gulgong. Other settlers came to the area, but it was the discovery by Tom Saunders in early 1870 of gold in workable amounts at nearby Red Hill that brought the boom times. Within three months, there were 500 hopefuls on the goldfields that spread through the area and had splendid and evocative names such as "Coming Event", "Perseverance", "Nil Desperandum" and "Happy Valley". By 1872 numbers had swelled to 20,000.

The town was described by Anthony Trollope in 1871 as two intersecting streets "in each of which every habitation had probably required but a few days for its erection. The fronts of the shops were covered with large advertisements, the names and the praises of the traders, as is customary now with all newfangled marts; but the place looked more like a fair than a town." (p.122)

Henry Lawson's poem "The Roaring Days" gives a vivid picture of the hopeful diggers on the goldfields:

> Their shining Eldorado,
> Beneath the Southern skies,
> Was day and night forever
> Before their eager eyes.
> The brooding bush, awakened,
> Was stirred in wild unrest,
> All the year a human stream
> Went pouring to the West.

Thomas Browne who wrote under the pen name of Rolf Boldrewood was Chief Magistrate and Warden of the goldfields from 1871 to 1881 and in his evenings wrote stories of the gold rush and bushranging. "The Miner's Right", first published in magazines in 1880 and 1881 described life on the goldfields. More successful was "Robbery Under Arms", an accurate telling of the lawlessness also found on the goldfields.

The cultural life of Gulgong was not neglected—miners wherever they were always seemed to put up a theatre and there always seemed to be ladies willing to travel to the back of beyond to entertain them. Perhaps it was the stories of actresses being showered with gold nuggets that lured them. Gulgong's Prince of Wales Opera House began life in 1872 as Cogdon's Assembly Rooms, reputedly the largest bark structure ever built. It was rebuilt in weatherboard with a timber floor and attracted performers such as Nellie Melba in its heyday.

By 1875, returns were diminishing and the diggers departed to new fields at Temora and Parkes. Mining continued in a minor way, but by 1880 Gulgong was reduced to 1,200 inhabitants. The advent of the railway in 1909 helped the district

Street scene, Gulgong c1870–75.

find markets for its wheat and wool and Gulgong became a quiet country town. Electricity arrived in 1923 and a much needed town water supply in 1933. By the 1950s, the town's streets were paved which brought to an end a favourite occupation of the locals—"specking" for gold. Previously, the roads had been top dressed with spoil from the goldfields and after rain small pieces of gold could be found glinting in the sunshine!

The First World War deeply affected Gulgong, as it did towns and villages throughout Australia—by 1917, through public subscriptions and fetes, the money had been raised and a design chosen from a competition for a memorial rotunda to commemorate the fallen from the district. The design by Albert E. Bates, Architect, of 121 Pitt Street, Sydney was chosen.

His very attractive rotunda "carried up in brick and cement" has a concrete dome supported on eight columns representing the six states and two territories of Australia. At the top of each pillar is a letter, the whole spelling out ANZAC and GPA (the Gulgong Progress Association). It was built by James Wildman and cost £244. Dedicated on 9 March 1918, it is one of the earliest war memorial rotundas in Australia.

Every visitor to Gulgong should see the War Memorial Rotunda in its attractive parkland setting. It reminds us of the sacrifice made by so many of those from small towns and the pride and vitality which made Gulgong a survivor of the "roaring days".

❖

bathurst
new south wales

The infant colony of Sydney was already running out of arable land by 1800 and expeditions were sent out to try to find a way west over the formidable barrier of the Blue Mountains. Explorers Blaxland, Wentworth and Lawson in 1813 and penetrated the bush as far as two kilometres west of present day Katoomba. At that point, they judged that they had accomplished their goal by marking out a road that would provide passage across the mountains. Surveyor George Evans followed and discovered the plains which he said would have "enough grass to support the stock of this colony for thirty years".

In 1815, Governor Macquarie with his artist John Lewin followed Evans's track to select a site for a new town on the plains. "Determined to have a good practicable Cart Road made with the least practicable delay", he selected sixty convicts "who had been a Certain Time in the Colony and who were also considered well behaved Men and entitled ... to some Indulgence". They were told they would be given conditional pardons if they finished the road—all 126 miles [202 km]—in six months; they achieved this herculean task and were set free.

Macquarie named his new town Bathurst after the Secretary of State for Colonies, Earl Bathurst. Each of the first settlers was granted 50 acres (20 hectares) of land, a servant, a cow, four bushels of wheat, a town allotment and twelve

months' provisions from the King's Stores—a generous start, although later they had to contend with a severe drought and the consequent economic recession.

Settlers had fossicked gold in creeks in the area in the early 1840s, but the Governor of New South Wales, Sir George Gipps, fearing the social upheaval of a gold rush, suppressed this information. All this was to change dramatically when Edward Hargraves found traces of gold in the Lewis Ponds Creek (which he later called Ophir) near Bathurst on 12 February 1851. Hargreaves talked up his finds in local hotels and within days the rush began. In May, The Bathurst Free Press prophesied that "there would be much immediate social confusion as the temperate and sober pleasures of domestic life were sacrificed for the dreamy and intoxicating but elusive expectation of a golden future." How true this was.

The population of Bathurst doubled during the 1850s and many of the handsome buildings seen today are evidence of the wealth pouring into the town. Ten years later the gold rush was over and Bathurst reverted to being the centre for the local pastoral industry.

Machattie Park in the centre of Bathurst is on the site of the original gaol and is named after Dr R. Machattie who served several times as Mayor and was instrumental in establishing the park. Facing the park is one of Australia's most imposing buildings, the Court House and its two wings which once housed the Postal and Telegraph offices. Designed by James Barnet, one of Australia's foremost Victorian architects, it was built in 1880 and forms a grand backdrop to the park.

Another architect who made a significant contribution was James Hine who was born in England and arrived in Australia in 1884. He practised in Bathurst for twelve years. As well as designing several major city buildings, he was responsible for the layout of Machattie Park and the design of the caretaker's cottage and the splendid band rotunda opened in 1890. The rotunda with its turned timber columns, timber brackets, frieze and turret is a very early example of the Arts and Crafts movement which James Hine no doubt brought with him from England. Hine moved to Western Australia in 1896 and continued his practice, finding time to submit entry no. 25 for the design of the new capital, Canberra. It was based on a series of circles and completely ignored the topography.

The park holds other treasures: the grand Crago Memorial Fountain with its encircling dolphins; the begonia house and fernery; and the cast iron Monroe memorial drinking fountain based on a design in MacFarlane's 1876 Example Book.

With its handsome Victorian buildings, Bathurst is Australia's oldest inland city. It is a centre for the pastoral industry, coal mining, manufacturing and education, enriched by the campuses of Charles Sturt University and several private schools.

❖

maitland
new south wales

The arrival of Governor Macquarie in New South Wales on 28 December 1809 began an era of development and expansion. A major part of this development took place in the Hunter Valley north of Sydney. Macquarie visited the area in January 1812, being rowed up the Hunter River as far as Raymond Terrace about 25 kilometres from the sea, where he noted the fertile alluvial flats on both sides. It was these river flats that the Victorian English author Douglas Jerrold later had in mind, when he said of Australian soil that "you need but to tickle it with a hoe to make it laugh with a harvest".

Macquarie paid another visit in July 1818, getting as far up the Hunter River as present day Maitland, which he named Wallis Plains in honour of the Commandant at Newcastle, the convict colony at the mouth of the River. Macquarie gave permission for four settlers to leave Sydney and farm the fertile land at Wallis Plains. They were soon followed by eleven "well behaved" convicts who were each allowed to take up 30 acres (75 hectares).

One of these convicts was the remarkable Molly Morgan, who first arrived in the colony in 1790 on board the *Neptune*, leaving behind two children. She had been sentenced to death for stealing yarn, but this was commuted to transportation. After five years in the colony, she persuaded the captain of the *Resolution* to take

her back to England. There she was reunited with her children and married Thomas Mare. This marriage did not last long; the ungallant Mr Mare had her rearrested and she was back in Sydney in 1803. Molly, who obviously had a way with men, moved in with an officer, but fell from grace again over the matter of some illegally branded cattle. Off she went to the penal colony at Newcastle where she was granted her ticket of leave in 1819.

Over time, Molly acquired a great deal of land at Wallis Plains, eventually owning most of the High Street. At sixty she married once again; Thomas Hunt was only 31 years old. She went on to organise the building of the school, the church and the hospital and, when she died at the age of seventy-three, she was known as "the Queen of the Hunter Valley".

The change of name from Wallis Plains to Maitland in 1835 was probably in honour of Sir Peregrine Maitland, a patron of the new Governor Darling.

By the 1840s, Maitland was a boom town. Its population in 1841 was exceeded only by Parramatta's and Sydney's, and by 1861 only Sydney was larger. Wool came to Maitland and nearby Morpeth from New England and goods from Sydney passed in the opposite direction. The opening of the rail link to Newcastle in 1857 gave a further boost to the thriving town.

Substantial buildings were appearing, some designed by well known architects. St John the Baptist Church built in 1846 was probably designed by Mortimer Lewis, but is much altered; Edmund Blacket designed St Mary's Church in 1867; and James Barnet the Post Office built in 1881. The new Town Hall designed by local architects Lee and Scobie quickly became the focus of local life. Meetings, including Edmund Barton speaking on his proposal for the federal constitution, dramatic performances, and concerts took place here. One spectacular event was the show put on by the Davis Vaudeville Company, the proposed highlight being a "flight by the Great Volteen" on a wire from the Town Hall to the pub across the road, achieved by holding a leather strap in his teeth. This was vetoed, so Volteen "flew" instead from the back wall of the Town Hall to the stage, rounding off the display with a trapeze act from the roof beams.

Maitland's racecourse became the West Maitland Park in 1884. Among many memorials in the park was the grand drinking fountain in memory of Mayor Richard Young who died in 1893. The fountain was unveiled on Empire Day 1896. The band rotunda, unique because it is decorated with wrought iron and not cast iron, was dedicated in 1908 after a great deal of deliberation by the Town Council and residents. No designer is named, but the columns were cast by Sims and Sons of Morpeth, so they may also have been responsible for the design. Gas was connected to the rotunda so that the bands had light for concerts in the summer evenings.

The town certainly needed a home for its bands, which had been playing since the middle of the 19th century. A brass band was present at the opening of a new bridge between East and West Maitland in 1852 and again at the completion of the railway in 1857. The Federal Band, active from the 1890s to the 1920s, was paid an annual fee to play in the park—on thirty-seven occasions in 1914—so the rotunda was well used. Today it sits quietly in its corner of the park surrounded by memorials and trees, a graceful and unusual example of bandstand architecture. ❖

goulburn
new south wales

Every now and again, there is someone in the right place at the right time. One such was Edmund Cooper Manfred and his right place was Goulburn in the late 19th century. Born in England in 1856, he travelled to Australia with his widowed mother in 1870. In Sydney, he studied architecture and surveying and worked in the office of E.T. Blacket who had designed the magnificent St Saviour's Cathedral in Goulburn. Manfred moved to Goulburn in 1879 and set up practice as an architect and surveyor. Within a couple of years, he was appointed Clerk of Works for St Saviour's, a position he retained until the building was completed in 1884. From 1880 until his retirement in 1914, he produced an enormous volume of work ranging from tiny cottages to the hospital, Town Hall, and Goulburn's first swimming pool.

His drawings were elegant and accurate and the buildings were accomplished and had a sense of *joie de vivre* which one likes to think echoed his personality. He was active in Goulburn in all sorts of ways. His obituary in the *Goulburn Evening Penny Post* of 21 February 1941 said he was 'a noted figure in Goulburn, and at one time or another was associated with practically all the public bodies'.

Goulburn, during Manfred's years of practice, had become a thriving centre of the fine wool industry and a major railway terminus with coach building workshops, breweries (one of which survives), foundries and flour mills. A reminder of Goulburn's wool industry heritage is the Big Merino, a very large replica said, not surprisingly, to be the world's largest concrete sheep. It towers above a highway services centre on the outskirts.

It did not take very long for Goulburn to become established after Charles Throsby, Hamilton Hume and Surveyor James Meehan explored the district in 1818. Meehan named the district the Goulburn Plains after Henry Goulburn, the Undersecretary for War and the Colonies—an interesting portfolio of responsibilities. Robert Dixon surveyed a site at the confluence of the Wollondilly and Mulwaree rivers and some huts, a lockup, court house and barracks were built. It soon became obvious that the town site would be flooded frequently, so the town was moved south to higher ground.

The town grew quickly. Surveyor General Mitchell wrote on 1 November 1836: "I continued my ride through the new Township in which although but a few years had elapsed since I had sketched its streets on paper, a number of houses had already been built."

By 1853, Dr Lang commented that he "deemed it the finest town in the interior of New South Wales". Goulburn by 1863 had become, by Royal letters patent, a bishopric, therefore a cathedral city, which meant that a grand cathedral was required. St Saviour's Cathedral is one of Blacket's best buildings. The siting is spectacular and the interior majestic—it must have been a great pleasure for Manfred to see its progress to completion.

Other substantial buildings were being built. The Post Office, a James Barnet design, was opened in 1881. The Court House, also by Barnet, opened in 1887. The Court House is opposite Belmore Park and in Belmore Park is one of Edmund Manfred's smallest, but most attractive designs—the band rotunda. Belmore Park has been central to the life of Goulburn since the city's beginnings, the site for the town market and a meeting place for picnics and sporting events. It was named Belmore Square in 1869 when Lord and Lady Belmore graced the celebrations for the completion of the railway from Sydney.

A big sports picnic was held in the park in 1897 to celebrate Queen Victoria's Diamond Jubilee. After the picnic, there was a surplus of £49 and this was put towards the construction of a bandstand to commemorate the Jubilee. After a grant of £75 from the Government was added, Manfred was approached to design a bandstand at a cost of £120. The design drawings still exist to show that Manfred's first two designs did not suit the Citizens and Band Committee, but they did, finally, accept Design No.3!

With its cupola, curved roof and delicate double-sided cast iron (as specified), it was built by Allen for £133 10 shillings. *The Goulburn Evening Penny Post* of 18 July 1899 reads: "The contractor was Mr. Arthur Allen of Goulburn, and he has carried out the work in a very satisfactory manner. He executed the carpentering, the ironwork was supplied by the Goulburn Engineering Works, Mr. H. Edwards did the brick and cement work, Mr. W. Stewart the painting and Mr. Lemon the plumbing."

Since it was declared open on 15 July 1899, the bandstand has given pleasure to the citizens of the second oldest inland city in Australia. ❖

singleton
new south wales

Architect John Wiltshire Pender was the most influential architect in the Hunter Valley in the second half of the 19th century. Born in Tobermory, Isle of Mull, in 1833, he was articled to James Ross and studied part-time at the Royal Academy of Inverness. His family came to Australia in 1855 and settled in Maitland 50km from Singleton, where Pender worked with his builder uncle in 1857.

John Pender's architectural practice, the first in the Hunter Valley, started in 1863 and was continued by family members until 1988—a very long-lived practice. He designed many buildings in the region—hotels, churches, banks and several handsome houses. Throughout his long career he was much involved in the life of the district, particularly in education. He campaigned for a technical college at Maitland, was one of the founders of Maitland Scientific and Historical Society and School of Arts, and was elected a life member of the Improvement Association in 1881.

One small and charming structure he designed is the bandstand at the Singleton Showground. It has had its share of ups and downs in a long life, having been relocated twice, suffered from vandalism, and lost its basement, probably during the move to the new Showground. The basement was originally clad in fake stonework and the upper level accessed via an internal ladder. The bandstand still has its beautifully detailed cast iron brackets and frieze. The bunches of grapes with vine leaves and tendrils on the frieze are a most appropriate decoration for Australia's early premier winegrowing region. All but one of the cast iron columns survive. Pender's cast iron designs were elegant and immaculately cast, as can be seen particularly on his grand two storey houses. By 1885, he had patented many of his designs, some of which bore his name "J.W. Pender, Maitland (11-5-1885)".

A meeting at the Royal Hotel in Singleton on 28 May 1868 decided to form an agricultural association that would buy land for a Showground. With admirable speed 4 ½ acres (1.8 hectares) were purchased in South Singleton, and fenced. Cattle and sheep pens were built; and later Pender designed pig pens, cattle sheds and sheep and fowl pens—a very versatile architect!

The first show was held on 27 August 1868, only three months after the land purchase! In 1874, another purchase brought the total showground land to 8 acres (3.2 hectares).

J.W. Pender designed the pavilion, an airy and attractive building, in May 1880 and on 1 June 1881 tenders were called for "the Erection and Completion of Band Pavilion, W. Closets and other improvements". From five tenders received, Richard Dalton's for the sum of £235 18 shillings 11 pence was accepted.

From the beginning, the bandstand was the focus for entertainment at the

Photo of Singleton Town Band, 1929.

shows. In 1896, H.B. Solomon submitted a proposal for entertainment on the two nights of the show—"a promenade concert, to consist of 7 or 8 members of the Singleton Amateur Orchestral Society and about 6 numbers by first class singers with changes for second night". The proposal was accepted and the concert went well—as reported in the local newspaper: "The Singleton Amateur Orchestra Society and several gentlemen vocalists ... presented a programme sufficient to satisfy the most exacting." The Singleton Town Band which has been playing continuously since 1878, one of the oldest in the state, if not Australia, played in the bandstand.

The bandstand is still well used. A musical group plays there on the monthly market day and musicians play at the Art Shows and Craft Shows held in the Pavilion. It remains a focal point in the Showground.

The grandstand, also designed by Pender, but later modified, completes an attractive set of buildings now in the care of a volunteer group.

More adjacent land was bought in 1881, but it was becoming obvious that an even larger area was needed. Sixteen acres (6.5 hectares) closer to the town centre were bought in 1908 for £800, and all the buildings, including the bandstand, were moved to the new site at the substantial cost of £2650. The first show at the new location took place on 15–16 September 1910. More land bought later brought the Showground to its present size.

The Singleton Show continues annually with just a few breaks. Only four have been missed since 1868—because of a bad drought, an Australia-wide rail strike, and for two years in the Second World War when the Showground was taken over by the Army.

If you go to the Show, in September, you will be entertained by riding events and admire beef and dairy cattle and poultry. There are sections for handcrafts, cooking, woodworking, horticulture and fine arts, but perhaps the most popular and unusual event for an agricultural show is the Annual Oak Australia Wife Carrying titles. Wife-carrying contests started in Finland in 1992 and Singleton has hosted them since 2005.

When you have enjoyed all the events, take time to look at the bandstand which has been part of the Showground for so long—a small but delightful example of Pender's architecture. ❖

glebe park
canberra

The first Europeans to see the site of Australia's capital were Doctor Charles Throsby and his overseer Joseph Wild in 1820, when they were searching for the Murrumbidgee River. They camped on what was later called the Limestone Plains, probably near Duntroon, climbed Black Mountain the next day, then followed the Molonglo River as far as the site of present day Queanbeyan. Throsby described the plain as "perfectly sound, well watered with extensive meadows of rich land on either side of the rivers".

Stockmen employed by J.J. Moore were the first to settle on these extensive meadows in 1824. They built huts on the Acton Peninsula, the site of the National Museum, and grazed cattle. Moore built a house there and by 1826 applied to buy the land, describing it as "situate at Canberry on the E. Bank of the river which waters Limestone Plains".

Another early settler was Charles Campbell whose overseer brought sheep to the Duntroon area in 1825. When Campbell, a Scot, arrived at Duntroon in 1835, he brought twelve Highland shepherds to the colony. By 1838, he was employing sixty to seventy free immigrant shepherds. He also arranged for a clergyman to tend to the religious needs of his human flock in the small village of Queanbeyan, and

in 1866 and proposed that the six colonies form a Federal Council to consider federation, ending bickering over tariffs between colonies and other complications of trade and borders, and replacing British control.

After several false starts, the Federal Convention of 2 March 1891 agreed on a two house parliament and the appointment of a Governor-General. Then the big question arose: where was this new Federal Parliament going to meet? The Melbourne Premiers' Conference in 1888 had agreed that the capital should be in New South Wales, more than 100 miles from Sydney, and have an area of 100 square miles. The draft Constitution of 1898 gave the future Federal Parliament the right to choose the site and Federal Parliament was to sit in Melbourne until this site was chosen.

Advertisements in provincial and city newspapers asked for suggestions and they poured in—45 of them. Alexander Oliver, a lawyer specialising in rural and maritime law was chosen to examine the most promising sites. Oliver inspected twenty-three of the forty-five sites which ranged from Armidale to Albury, and held public enquiries at fourteen.

Oliver's criteria were that the capital should have an invigorating climate, should be accessible and have fertile soil and topography suitable for the construction of "a beautiful and commodious city". King O'Malley, the larger than life Federal Member for Tasmania, was instrumental in the search for the capital's site and with John Gale, the proprietor of *The Queanbeyan Age* newspaper, supported Canberra as being the best place. Gale read a paper entitled: "Dalgety or Canberra, Which?" to a public meeting in Queanbeyan on 3 July 1907. With its "9 factors of logic" and "indisputable facts", the paper was sent to every member of the Federal Parliament and six state parliaments and to other people of influence. It obviously influenced them, as Canberra was voted the site in 1909 for the future Federal capital.

On Wednesday 12 March 1913, 500 official guests were on hand to hear what the new capital would be named. It was no great surprise when Lady Denman, the wife of the Governor General announced that it would be called "Canberra—the accent is on the Can". Lord Denman, in his speech, said "here a city may arise where those responsible for the government of this country in the future may seek and find inspiration in its noble buildings, its broad avenues, its shaded parks and sheltered gardens."

O'Malley was given the post of Federal Minister of Home Affairs in 1910. He believed the design of Canberra should be open to competition and early in 1911 the Federal Government gave approval for a design competition with O'Malley leading a panel of experts to assess the entries. O'Malley would make the final decision. This did not go down well with architects and other experts, but he had his forceful way.

began the construction of a school and church, St John the Baptist, in what is now the Canberra suburb of Reid. Campbell also donated land for a rectory and its glebe. The rectory was built in 1871–73 and the surrounding land was planted with elms, some of which survive to this day. By this time, the farm land on the Limestone Plains had been bought up and divided into large stations, with some smaller farms on the river flats.

In the wider world of the Australian colonies, agitation for Federation was being heard, led by Sir Henry Parkes. Parkes became New South Wales Colonial Secretary

Designs were due in Melbourne on 31 January 1912 with prizes of £1750, £750 and £500. Clause 18 of the competition conditions stated that "the premiated designs shall become the property of the government for its unrestricted use, either in whole or in part." This clause opened the way to later dreadful travesties of the winning design.

Walter Burley Griffin's prizewinning design rendered exquisitely on silk by his wife, Marion Mahony, was a simple, elegant scheme which responded to the landscape. The three local mountains would be the terminations of the major axes, the major buildings would dominate from their positions on the lower hills and the Molonglo River would be dammed to form a lake linking the northern municipal and military area with the southern parliamentary area.

King O'Malley thought it was a wonderful scheme, but as in any competition, there were those who hated it. Eventually, O'Malley referred the three winning plans to a departmental board for advice and, as is usual with boards, it came up with a concoction of various bits of various schemes bearing little resemblance to the Burley Griffin plan. This was approved by O'Malley and sent to Walter Burley Griffin for his comments. His reaction was to come to Australia from his home in the United States to try to sort things out. While gaining some concessions from the bureaucrats, he finally gave up the struggle in 1920 with his dream only partially realised.

One of the shaded parks and sheltered gardens extolled by Lord Denman in his Canberra dedication speech in 1913 is Glebe Park near the city centre. Glebe Park is a remnant of the 40 hectare glebe of St John's Church, some of the shelter being provided by those elms planted before Federation.

It was only after public agitation to preserve the trees, that the park was officially defined and named on 14 December 1983 and listed by the National Trust (ACT) and the Australian Heritage Commission.

Formal landscaping with avenues of trees and generous lawns was designed to give an "English feeling" to the park, which includes a rotunda, fences and gates with stone piers named after prominent Canberra people or historic places. It was officially opened on Canberra Day 12 March 1989.

The rotunda is a prominent feature which sits nicely in this formal setting on an expanse of lawn backed by magnificent trees. Columns supporting an octagonal slate roof and a corrugated iron veranda are references to the style of early cottages. Designed by architects Philip Leeson and Peter Freeman of Peter Freeman and Partners, Design Architects of Canberra, it is a very popular and well used feature of a very attractive park. ❖

fitzroy gardens
melbourne

Australia's earliest bandstand can be found in Fitzroy Gardens. This classical rectangular building with square columns, entablature and pediment has been there since 1864—much earlier than the next oldest, the bandstand in Elder Park, Adelaide built in 1882. Designed by George Dodd and perhaps built by George or James Duncan, it cost £360 5 shillings. For many years it was a music venue—but on Sundays in colonial times only sacred music was allowed.

To have such a building in an established park so early says much about the rapid growth of Melbourne. The camp on the shores of Port Philip was formally named Melbourne and surveyed in 1837. By 1848, 64 acres (26 hectares) had been set aside as a reserve to be called Fitzroy Square after Sir Charles Fitzroy, Governor of New South Wales from 1846 to 1851 and Governor-General of the Australian Colonies from 1851 to 1855.

Described disparagingly as "two sandy ridges with a ravine between them", the park was fenced and gated against wandering stock by 1857, when a development plan was prepared by Edward La Trobe Bateman for the Melbourne Council. Bateman, who had studied architecture in England, was a friend of the pre-Raphaelite painters Holman Hunt, Rossetti and Ford Madox Brown who farewelled him when he sailed for Melbourne on the *Windsor*. It was this occasion that inspired Brown's famous

The Kiosk, c1910.

painting "The Last of England". Bateman made many sketches of the goldfields and later worked for Reed and Bums, architects.

Bateman's plan showed a curved roadway at the north end of the park and winding paths crossing the creek which runs down what was once the "ravine". Melbourne Council thought Bateman's plan was too elaborate and in 1862 it was redesigned by Deputy Surveyor-General Clement Hodgkinson, who controlled every aspect of the development of Fitzroy Gardens. He selected trees, flowers, statues and fountains, hired staff, supervised earthworks and even ordered shovels. Each morning, he walked through Fitzroy Gardens on his way to his office. He would then issue his orders and, on his way home, would check that they had been carried out. Hodgkinson, described in *The Illustrated Melbourne Post* as "that most tasteful of amateur gardeners", was assisted by gardener James Sinclair who came from Scotland in 1854.

Hodgkinson's design showed diagonal paths crossing the creek with statuary at their intersections. Quick growing blue gums and wattles provided windbreaks against the dust of the streets and the major paths were lined with elms. This was a great improvement on the situation as reported in *The Argus* on 12 July 1858: "nothing was planted in the ground, save such dead animals and cast off wearing apparel as the people in the neighbourhood had no use for."

The 1870s were a high period for the Fitzroy Gardens. People came to listen to the band and stroll along the broad shady paths with their vistas of statues and fountains. Tree ferns and willows had been planted along the creek running through the centre. The neo-Classical circular Temple of the Winds was added in 1873.

N.M. Bickford was appointed Inspector of Metropolitan Bailiffs and Overseer of Parklands in 1872. His duties included the maintenance and policing of Fitzroy Gardens. Plain clothes police patrolled to prevent "flower thieves", larrikins and

preachers. He remained until John Guilfoyle, who had redesigned the Botanic Gardens, set about redesigning Fitzroy Gardens. Lots of trees were removed and colourful carpet bedding schemes were installed which were very popular with Victorian-era visitors.

Buildings added at this time were a nursery for all those bright carpet bedding flowers, which also supplied other gardens, and a kiosk in the centre which had tea rooms, a band stand, a residence for the curator and toilets. That rustic structure sadly burnt down in 1960.

J.T. Smith became curator in 1921 and during his time many trees were removed and replaced with lawns planted with fewer gingko trees, palms and silver birches. The Spanish Mission style Conservatory was built during the Depression in the midst of much controversy. Captain Cook's cottage (actually his parents' house) arrived from Great Ayrton in 1934 and an 18th century garden was added in 1970.

The Fitzroy Gardens are on the Victorian Heritage Register as an important remnant of the city's 19th century garden heritage. With their restored statuary, fountains, shady pathways, Temple of the Winds and the serene bandstand where a visitor can sit and contemplate the vista of lawns and tree-lined avenues, the Gardens are a much loved and frequented green space in the centre of the city. ❖

prahran
melbourne

The Grattan Gardens in the Melbourne suburb of Prahran contain a mystery: an ornate bandstand that appears to have been imported many years ago. No one knows who donated it or when it arrived in Grattan Gardens in all its elaborate Eastern splendour. The design does not appear in Scottish or local cast iron catalogues. A search through Prahran Council Minutes of 1885 to 1895 (apart from 1892 and 1893 that are missing) reveals no mention of financing or building a bandstand.

The earliest known evidence of its existence is a Melbourne and Metropolitan Board of Works plan of 1896 which shows it in a typically Victorian era garden layout of winding paths and flower beds.

Prahran was the name given to the area by George Langhorne who was appointed to form a mission station in Port Phillip in 1836. The name is probably a compound of two Aboriginal words meaning "land surrounded by water"—a reference to the swampy land.

The first sales of Crown land to settlers were in May 1850. Prahran became a municipality in 1855 with twenty five streets. Grattan Street was named after Henry Grattan, an Irish patriot, by Irish doctor O'Mullane who bought a portion of Section 41—7 acres (3 hectares)—which became known as Mullane's paddocks.

Public parks and gardens took a long time to appear, but in early 1884 to rectify

Victorian era layout appears in a 1914 photograph with the bandstand in its original place on its brick base, with its cast iron balustrades intact. Massed flower displays spell out "Advance Australia" and other patriotic symbols.

At the end of the First World War, there were 32 acres (13 hectares) of public land in Prahran. By the end of the next decade, this had doubled, most being dedicated to specialised uses—tennis courts, bowling greens, playgrounds. During the Second World War, many parks were dug up to provide shelter trenches, but by 1944 they had been filled in and the lawns were back.

The bandstand was relocated twice. The first move was in the late 1980s when it was rebuilt at the southern end of the gardens on a new red brick base with its original cast iron balustrade replaced by a modern metal balustrade. The bandstand now sits in the northern end of the gardens on a concrete slab, where, despite the indignities it has suffered over the last century, it retains its unique character as the only example of this style of cast iron bandstand decoration in Australia. ❖

this deficiency, Prahran Municipal Council decided at a special meeting that a loan of £12,000 be floated to buy land for parks. At a meeting in the Town Hall on 19 July 1884, the Council heard the protests of those who thought it was far too much money. The Council went ahead anyway—with the recommendation of the Parks Committee that the loan be used for "purchasing grounds for parks and pleasure gardens". The Council had already bought some land in secret.

In quick order, land that came to form the Victoria Gardens, Toorak Park and Prahran Reserve, now known as Grattan Gardens, was purchased. Lady Loch, the wife of the Governor of Victoria, opened the parks on 7 August 1885. "I declare the lands of the city of Prahran known as Toorak Park, the Victoria Gardens and the Prahran Reserve to be dedicated to public use and enjoyment as pleasure gardens and places of enjoyment".

Prahran was expanding rapidly and became a centre for brewing, baking and manufacturing, producing clothing and furniture. The parks were well used by people working in the area. As in many parks and gardens, the occasional undesirable element crept in. On 4 January 1895, the Council was asked to take the necessary steps to suppress larrikinism in the public gardens. Council minutes report that "statements were made to Mr Fetherston of disgraceful conduct of certain persons."

The Gardens were extended in 1909 and the stone gates and fencing were added at a cost £327 8 shillings. The gates are still there, but not the fences. The

beaufort
victoria

By the early 1840s, the land to the west of Melbourne was opening up. The first settlers in the area of the future Beaufort were brothers R. and J.M. Hamilton, and K.W. Kirkland, who established Trawalla Station in 1838. Regular traffic with Melbourne began in 1847 when a gig with room for two passengers began passing through Fiery Creek on its way to Portland in the Western District.

Fiery Creek, four kilometres from Beaufort, was the site of a modest gold rush. Gold was found there in 1852 and by 1854 there were four townships—Fiery Creek, Yam Holes Creek, View Point and Southern Cross. Alluvial gold was gone by the 1860s, but deep reef mining continued until 1914.

Meanwhile, Beaufort was developing. The town was surveyed in 1857 and the first building lots sold in 1858. The flour mill was built in 1865 and the railway arrived in 1874 as the surrounding district grew. There is a theory about the origin of the town's name, that it was named after Admiral Beaufort who designed his eponymous wind scale in 1805.

Whatever its origin, it is a grand name and it has a grand bandstand to match. A bandstand was first proposed in early 1903 by C.W. Jones, secretary of the already well established band. Mr Jones was not happy about young bandsmen having to practise at the pub. The band president, J.R. Wotherspoon, thought a bandstand was an excellent idea and so did the citizens of Beaufort who by April had raised £80, enough for a rotunda and a remarkable result for a community of about two thousand.

With great speed, the site was selected, a competition for the design was launched, and the winner chosen—architects Clegg and Miller of Ballarat. By this time, £180 had been raised—a princely sum reflected in the winning design. The bandstand was built on the site of the tiny office for the weighbridge that weighed goods before they were transferred to the railway. The bandstand's face brick base housed the new weighbridge office and cast iron columns supported a roof with a tower and clock, a rarity among Australian bandstands. The chosen builders, Messrs Stevenson Bros., started work and on 23 September 1903 the foundation stone was laid.

A decision had been made that the rotunda should be a memorial to Queen Victoria with an appropriate plaque. One plaque on the base reads "AD1903. Erected by the residents of Beaufort and district in commemoration of the glorious reign of her late Majesty Queen Victoria". On 2 December 1903, the Lord Mayor of Melbourne, Sir Malcolm McEarchen, performed the opening ceremony, Lady McEarchen ran up the flag, and Mrs Bridges started the clock.

In his speech, Sir Malcolm said that it was the first memorial in Victoria to the memory of the late queen. A second plaque reads: "The clock that surmounts this building was presented by Rear Admiral Bridges of Trawalla". Rear Admiral Walter Bridges joined the Royal Navy in 1856. He was on the Australia Station from 1871 to 1880 and during that time he met and married Caroline Wilson, the daughter of John Wilson of Woodlands, a property in the Wimmera. When he retired from the service in 1887, Mr Bridges bought Trawalla, built a handsome two-storeyed house and became a successful pastoralist.

The bandstand went through many vicissitudes before it was returned to its original state nearly a century later. The brick base at one stage was painted white and in 1979, the National Trust, which had classified the bandstand in 1976, announced a grant of $1,000 to remove the paint, the shire council offering a further $500. Neither of these grants appears to have been taken up.

In 1985, the Council put in a request for $4,000 to the Ministry of Planning and Environment—the Shire Engineer's estimate for maintenance, roof repairs and provision of stairs. Access until then had been through a trapdoor in the floor.

This request was presumably denied, as in 1986 an application was made to the Central Goldfields Restoration Fund which responded with the offer of a $10,000 low interest loan for restoration of the original colours. This offer was not taken up either.

In 1992, *The Ballarat Courier* stated that $15,850 was needed for the restoration. A public meeting was organised by the band committee and, at last, the money was raised to do major repairs, including a centre pole to support the clock mechanism.

The bandstand in its restored glory remains a focus of the town—decorated with fairy lights at Christmas, and with its garden, a pleasant place to stop on the highway west through the prosperous farmland of the Western Districts.

ballarat
victoria

Band music has been part of the life of Ballarat since its earliest days. A brass band played at the meeting at Bakery Hill on 1 November 1854 which led eventually to the rebellion at the Eureka Stockade on 3 December.

The Ballarat City Brass Band has a long history starting in 1887 when Thomas Bulch and some musical friends formed Bulch's Model Brass Band which in 1900 became the Ballarat City Brass Band that we know today. Bulch was also partly responsible for the inauguration of the Royal South Street Contest on 15 October 1900 in which nine bands competed. On 31 October 1903, *The Sydney Morning Herald* reported that a parade of 500 bandsmen from seventeen bands assembled at the Prince of Wales Square and played the "Southern Cross" march before going off to the competitions—it must have been deafening!

Ballarat quite rightly became known as the band music capital of Australia. The Ballarat City Brass Band continues to play as does the Ballarat Memorial Concert Band which was formed in about 1920 by a returned soldier, Private H.J. Norman McWilliams. Originally restricted to returned soldiers, membership was later extended to all service people and it is now open to all musicians.

When the bandsmen of Ballarat heard of the heroic last music played by the bandsmen of the *Titanic* when she sank in 1912, they decided to honour them with

a commemorative bandstand. It stands in Sturt Street—an attractive and unusual structure. The wind vane is a model of the *Titanic*.

The bandstand was designed by local architect George W. Clegg, who was responsible for many buildings in Ballarat and central and western Victoria. The Queen Alexandra bandstand further up Sturt Street built in 1908 and the grand bandstand at Beaufort, Victoria (see p.75) are also his work.

The *Titanic* bandstand, erected in 1913, has an almost oriental feeling to its elaborate roof structure. The columns and brackets are from the Eagle Foundry in Ballarat. It is unique among the bandstands of Australia in being a memorial to the *Titanic* bandsmen. The citizens of Broken Hill attempted to build such a bandstand, but could not raise sufficient funds by public subscription. With the money raised they had to settle for a broken column memorial that now stands in Sturt Park in Broken Hill.

The bandstand in Ballarat is one of many buildings and monuments in Sturt Street that reflect the prosperity generated by the gold which came in enormous quantities from the mines of East Ballarat.

Ballarat grew rapidly after gold was discovered in August 1851. West Ballarat was surveyed and designated a township in 1852 and by the 1860s the main streets were lined with substantial buildings. The grand Town Hall was built between 1859 and

1870; on "the Corner"—the colloquial name of an outdoor informal stock exchange—the Unicorn Hotel was built in 1866, replacing the 1856 timber building. *Australia's First Century* describes the scene: "Here the share brokers may be seen transmitting their business in the open street, and on busy days stretching right across to the gardens that adorn the middle, buying and selling, shouting and gesticulating as if their lives depended on it, as their livelihoods most undoubtedly do" (p.184). Her Majesty's Theatre built in 1875 in Lydiard Street was originally called the Academy of Music, the word "theatre" then being considered rather risqué. It has been the home of the Royal South Street Society of band music fame and the Grand National Eisteddfod since 1896, the oldest continuously operating purpose built theatre in Australia.

Lake Wendouree and the Botanic Gardens were developed from swampland on the western edge of Ballarat in the 1860s. Mark Twain was greatly impressed with the fact that "this little town has a park of 326 acres [132 hectares], a flower garden of 83 acres [34 hectares], with an elaborate and expensive fernery in it and some costly and unusually fine statuary; and an artificial lake covering 600 acres equipped with a fleet of 200 shells, small sail boats, and little steam yachts." (p.136)

The citizens flocked to their park to picnic, sail and listen to a band in a bandstand. It is still very popular with today's citizens. In 1922, George Clegg built a bandstand at the water's edge. This was a more rustic structure with sturdy volcanic stone piers, timber brackets and a tiled roof.

Ballarat managed to continue to prosper after the last mine closed in 1918. The city had developed many secondary industries during the "golden years"—iron foundries, flour mills, woollen mills and services for the surrounding farmland—and this continues today. The grand buildings remain and Ballarat is still the attractive, prosperous city it has been since colonial times. ❖

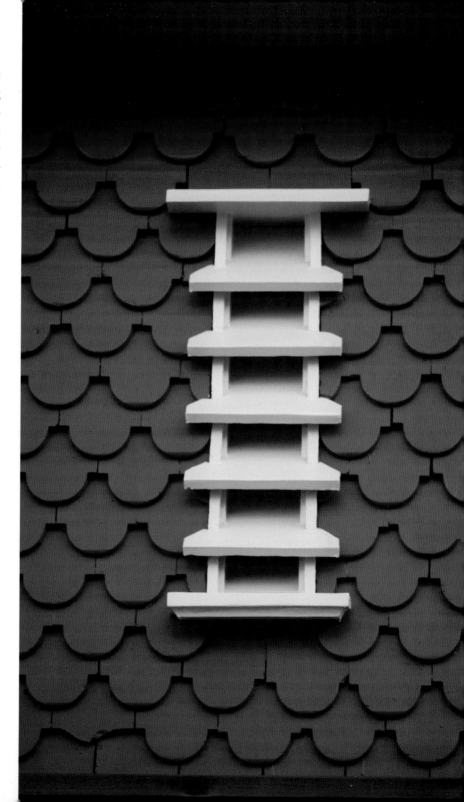

johnstone park
geelong, victoria

On the shores of Corio Bay just inside the entrance to Port Phillip, Geelong was for most of the 19th century the fifth largest town in Australia. There were two reasons for this—wool and gold.

Several early explorers saw the site of Geelong, but it was John Batman, an entrepreneurial son of convict parents, arriving from Van Diemen's Land (Tasmania) in 1835, who camped at Indented Head near Corio Bay and first saw the possibilities for settlement. He then went on to the new settlement of Melbourne. Returning to Van Diemen's Land, he wrote a letter to Governor Arthur, telling the Governor of his supposed contract with Port Phillip Aborigines and his plan to "civilise the natives" there. Although he was told his "contract" was null and void, Batman's brother and family and John Holder Wedge went to Port Phillip, followed by a flood of settlers from Van Diemen's Land to Melbourne and to Corio Bay.

By 1838, the town of Geelong had been surveyed. It had a reliable water supply from the Barwon River, surrounding land suitable for agriculture, but most importantly, a good site for a port to service the burgeoning wool industry of the Western District, where graziers moving down from the north had already settled.

Wool was the foundation of Geelong's prosperity in the 19th century, except during the brief period of the Ballarat gold rush in the 1850s. The development of the

wool industry made the Australian colonies less economically dependent on England. Geelong became the main wool port for the Western District. Before long some of the wool remained in Victoria to be turned into sturdy textiles in the grand stone woollen mills of Geelong, the first built in 1868. Other industries became established in Geelong—rope works, tanneries, paper mills.

The Ballarat gold rush boosted the prosperity of Geelong as it did Melbourne's. Geelong was the port with the easiest access to the goldfields and money poured into the town. "The whole town of Geelong is in hysterics," reported the Melbourne *Argus*. "Gentlemen foaming at the mouth, ladies fainting and children throwing somersaults." After the excitement of the rush abated, Geelong was left a legacy of handsome public and business buildings.

Geelong called itself "Pivot City" in the 1880s, because it was the hub for shipping and rail to Melbourne. But proximity to Melbourne meant that one centre inevitably was going to develop at the expense of the other. Melbourne prevailed, helped by

Corio Bay's sandbar which hindered ships coming into the harbour and had to be dredged regularly. Nevertheless, Geelong's rail and port facilities continued to attract industry. Proclaimed a city in 1910, Geelong developed into a major manufacturing centre.

Geelong has always had generous areas of parkland. Governor La Trobe had 55 acres (22 hectares) set aside for "ornamental and public garden grounds" when he visited in 1848. In 1867, 13 acres (5 hectares) of this land was made a public park named Johnstone Park in honour of the mayor. *The Geelong Advertiser*, first published in 1840, described it as a handsome little park.

A band rotunda built in 1875 did not last, and in 1915, newly elected Mayor Howard Hitchcock, at his second council meeting, moved that a public competition be held to beautify Johnstone Park. Hitchcock was an indefatigable promoter of Geelong; he was also interested in the arts and horticulture.

The prize was won by a young architect, Percy Everett, in association with the architectural firm of Laird and Buchan. His axial design focussed on key surrounding buildings and included a splendid Art Nouveau bandstand he designed to be placed in the centre of the park. Everett was a committed modernist and his bandstand design featured a strong buttressed rendered concrete base and slim columns supporting a dramatic curved pressed metal roof with four corner turrets and topped by a tall flagpole. Originally, the bandstand was in the middle of a small lake, but this has long since been replaced by flower beds.

The money for the bandstand was donated by Howard Hitchcock and it was dedicated to the memory of his mother. It was built by Bernard Murphy in 1919–20. Six thousand attended the opening and the Returned Services Band played musical selections. The party went on into the evening when the park's new lighting system was turned on.

Percy Everett also won the design competition for a Peace Memorial in the form of a civic hall. The foyer was built, but the hall never eventuated, which is a shame, as the foyer is a splendid piece of architecture. Everett went on to become Chief Architect of the Victorian Public Works Department and his office produced many striking "modern" public buildings.

An interesting postscript is that the Johnstone Park rotunda has an imitator in Yeo Park in Ashfield, Sydney. Built in 1929, it is the result of a design competition with the specific requirement that it be "based on the Geelong prototype". Ashfield Council's Engineer, Mr Reeves, had inspected parks in Victoria while on leave, so I suspect it was he who admired the Johnstone Park rotunda and wanted one just like it for Yeo Park. It is not surprising, therefore, that the winning design was identical apart from minor details. ❖❖

walhalla
victoria

The approach to the old gold mining town of Walhalla is suitably otherworldly. The forested road through the Baw Baw Ranges in northern Gippsland circles and climbs until suddenly arriving at a tiny settlement, clinging to the sides of a creek that winds through a deep gully.

Gold was discovered in this remote place in December 1862 by four intrepid prospectors—Edward (Ned) Stringer, William McGregor, William Griffiths and William Thompson. Word quickly spread and by February 1863 a hundred miners were panning for alluvial gold in what became known as Stringer's Creek.

Other prospectors were searching for the mother lode of this alluvial gold and in January 1863 an immense quartz lode was discovered on the mountainside on the western side of the creek. So much gold came from this lode, named Cohen's Line of Lode, that the most successful mine, the Long Tunnel Extended, became the fifth richest in Australia with a yield of 144,000 ounces of gold.

The tiny settlement which had been struggling with drought, fires and rain began to prosper. The main difficulty was access—a precipitous track known as Campbell's Track was the only way in. Bullock teams carried in everything needed in the settlement—machinery for the mines and even "human cargo"—some of the first women and children to come to the settlement travelled in gin cases strapped to the pack saddles.

A proper road was desperately needed to bring in heavy crushing batteries to extract the gold from the ore. The main obstacle on the route to the diggings was the Thompson River. With the help of government grants, a road was built and a bridge opened for traffic on 25 January 1864.

How Stringer's Creek became Walhalla is something of a mystery. One contender is Captain John Johnson, a local squatter who in a conversation with a mine manager,

Henry Rosales, is said to have likened the site to the home of the Norse heroes. Another version is that Rosales came up with the name himself. In true Australian fashion, the name came to be pronounced "Woller" by the locals.

The indefatigable Anthony Trollope visited Walhalla in early 1872. He and a friend rode there accompanied by a mounted policeman and he was taken by "its peculiar beauty ... The buildings ... lie along the stream, or are perched up on low altitudes among the trees." He was impressed by the fact that there was a piano in his hotel sitting room and a billiard table and, having experienced the terrible road into Walhalla, he admired the enterprise of the people who got them there. He also found that the people were courteous and kind, their children were well educated and there were many churches.

The Walhalla Brass Band played an important role in the life of the town. *The Walhalla Chronicle* commented in August 1883 that the Walhalla Brass Band had been 'an institution there for many years'. In 1885, it became the Mountaineer Brass Band and in 1890 donned smart uniforms.

Cricket was popular and home games were played on a ground 200 metres above the town. The ground was established by efforts of the local miners, who removed the top of a hill with their picks and shovels. At a match at Easter 1907, Australian test captain, Warwick Armstrong, made a bet that he would hit a six into the yard of the Star Hotel far below. He lost his bet, as he was caught on the boundary after making 12 runs.

Another site with extremely steep access was the cemetery on the eastern side of the creek. Pall bearers needed to be very fit and the graves themselves required pick and shovel work to hack out a reasonably level site.

In 1896, the Mountaineer Brass Band held a competition for the design of a band rotunda. F. Meyers of the local photographic firm was the winner. *The Walhalla Chronicle* of 3 July 1896 commented that "the rotunda will be quite an ornament to the junction end of town, and it will be found that property in its immediate neighbourhood will not deteriorate in value as was anticipated by those who were opposed to the erection of the building." A tender of £85 17s 6d was let and on the evening of 29 October 1896 completion of the rotunda was celebrated by a torchlight procession followed by a concert in the recently constructed Oddfellows Hall.

The 1880s and 90s were Walhalla's heydays. Fifteen hotels, two breweries, thirty stores and a 500-pupil school served a population of about 4,500. The gold mines produced great wealth. It is estimated that between 1863 and 1913 about 55 tons of gold came from Walhalla's reefs. But as is most gold mines, the effort to mine the remaining ore body became uneconomical and one by one the mines closed, the last, the Long Tunnel, ceasing work in 1913. The long awaited railway line eventuated in 1910, too late to be of value. Gradually, the town shut its doors. Miners left for the Wonthaggi coalfields or the gold mines in Kalgoorlie and at the beginning of the First World War many signed up for the armed forces.

Buildings were dismantled and taken to other towns. The brick vault of the Bank of Victoria can still be seen isolated on its otherwise vacant block—the rest of the building was re-erected in Moe. *The Walhalla Chronicle* closed in 1915, the Police Station in 1931, the railway in 1944 and the school in 1965. Fires in 1945 and 1951 and a devastating flood in 1952 destroyed many of the remaining buildings—but not the bandstand.

Maybe Walhalla would have disappeared altogether and become a myth like its namesake, if it had not been for residents who in 1945 started the Walhalla Improvement League—a very early community heritage preservation organisation. The name was changed to the Heritage and Development League in 2000 and it has been instrumental in preserving the remaining buildings, opening a museum and shop, and running ghost tours.

Walhalla is now a popular tourist destination and those who venture down those winding roads can ride the Walhalla Goldfields Railway which runs 4.5 kilometres to the Thompson River, take a tour in the Long Tunnel Extended Mine, and walk along Stringer's Creek through the old town, stopping to admire the Mountaineer Brass Band Rotunda still standing sturdily on the creek bank. ❖

st david's park
hobart

Sometimes it is an advantage to be small. Hobart, the capital of the smallest state, is a compact city. It doesn't trickle off in all directions like the mainland capitals. The centre can be seen in its entirety, enclosed by headlands either side or the looming presence of Mount Wellington behind. Its size attracts people—they appreciate its natural environment—it is the city where the "Green Movement" began. Its people are friendly and creative, but it had a difficult beginning as a convict settlement.

Hobart Town was not the first choice for a settlement in Van Diemen's Land. In 1803, Lieutenant John Bowen and his party decided that Risdon Cove further up the Derwent River was a satisfactory place. Risdon Cove was quickly found to be unsuitable and the Lieutenant Governor, Lieutenant Colonel David Collins, moved the settlement to its present position. He called it Hobart Town after the Secretary of State for the Colonies. It was a deepwater port which became important for the Southern Ocean whalers and sealers who were a lawless lot.

Governor Macquarie visited from Sydney in 1811. He found it in a "wretched state" and immediately ordered a survey. The resulting town plan was much the same as today's layout.

St David's Park was the burial ground from the beginning of settlement. Collins, who died in 1810, was buried there under the altar of a small timber church. The burial

The *Mercury's* report of 22 December goes on to say that the "Reserves Committee of Council ... submitted the plan of the bandstand proposed to be erected (which provides for a small shop underneath for the sale of soft drinks etc.) and recommended it be approved, that tenders be invited immediately".

Alderman Rogers said he hoped there would be no unnecessary opposition to the scheme and that "they wanted a bandstand in keeping with the park". Alderman Lamprill was opposed to the idea of the shop and thought the price was too high. The idea of the shop was dropped and the Mayor's suggestion that the bandsmen be consulted about the suitability of the design was adopted.

Hobart did get a bandstand in keeping with the park. Designed by the City Surveyor and Architect, Conway L. Clark, the zinc clad domed roof is supported by paired columns with a timber balustrade on a stone base. It cost £990, including £212 to provide storage on the ground floor. The ceiling was "specially treated to preserve the acoustic qualities". Built by Gillham Bros, the bandstand rests on a stonework base by E.S. Slevin.

The Classical style was appropriate, as Hobart had retained many of its early buildings. There is little Victorian or Federation architecture and this is due to Tasmania's history. There were financial difficulties after the cessation of convict transportation, a recession in the 1880s and 90s, and because of its isolation Tasmania missed out on the effects of the gold boom in Victoria.

Mark Twain described Hobart when he visited in 1895: "It is an attractive town. It sits on low hills that slope to the harbour ... it is the neatest town the sun shines on ... all the aspects are tidy, and all a comfort to the eye; the modestest cottage looks combed and brushed, and has its vines, its flowers, its neat fence, its neat gate, its comely cat asleep on the window ledge."

Hobart has remained "a comfort to the eye" and more and more visitors appreciate its Georgian buildings. The warehouses in Salamanca Place, which are a backdrop to one of Australia's liveliest markets, Henry Jones' sandstone jam factory— now a boutique hotel—and the Tasmanian Museum are outstanding examples.

Hobart is a creative place and its modest size has much to do with this. The arts flourish, no more spectacularly than in the Museum of Old and New Art— MONA—the creation of multi-millionaire David Walsh. Designed by architect Nonda Katsalidis, it is full of idiosyncratic, interesting and downright odd exhibits. MONA hosts cultural events throughout the year.

Hobart has a "still centre" in St David's Park. Stately trees, dignified monuments and the serene bandstand provide a peaceful place to contemplate the history of a small city which has seen great changes, yet preserves a close connection with its past.

ground, described in the 1820s as a place of great beauty, was not consecrated as an Anglican Church burial ground until 1823. In 1838, after the small timber church blew down, Lieutenant Governor John Franklin built a grand sandstone monument over Collins's grave. There are many other monuments to early governors and settlers in the park.

By the time of its closure in 1872, the burial ground had deteriorated. Collapsed graves and weeds made a suitable hiding place for ne'er do wells. Eventually, in 1920, the Anglican Church handed the cemetery to Hobart City Council to be used as a recreation ground. Many remains were reinterred in Cornelian Bay Cemetery and headstones were set in stone walls around the park. Some memorials were restored.

On 22 December 1925, *The Hobart Mercury* reported that "For some time since 1923 there has been an agreement in operation between the City Council and the Tasmanian Band Association whereby, until the Council provides the bands with a rotunda in St David's Park, it is subsidising the bands to the extent of £260 a year." Bands would play at the Beaumaris Zoo and other venues until the layout of St David's Park was completed.

city park
launceston, tasmania

As the second oldest public park in Australia, City Park in Launceston has been giving pleasure to young and old for a very long time. Established as a government garden for food in 1806, it was progressively planted with trees and plants sent by the Royal Society in England. Some of the trees survive to this day.

The Launceston Horticultural Society was formed in 1838 and given land adjacent to the garden for a botanical garden. This land was handed over to the Launceston Council in 1863 and became known as the People's Park then, later, City Park.

Among the structures in the park is a magnificent Macfarlane's Foundry drinking fountain and canopy—the Jubilee Fountain, presented to the city by the children of Launceston and erected in 1897 to commemorate the Golden Jubilee of Queen Victoria. The park is now also home to a conservatory, a monkey enclosure, and a rotunda.

The rotunda is built of timber. Timber columns with ogee shaped arches and fretwork infills are set off by a curved metal roof and ogee dome. The same style of fretwork forms the balustrades—the whole having a distinctly Indian feel. It was built to the plan of the City Surveyor, at the cost of £200 in 1908.

It is known as the Lithgow Rotunda in honour of Alexander Lithgow, a composer of band music and so widely known that in the USA he was called the "Sousa of the Antipodes". He composed music for silent films and was conductor and founder of the Launceston Concert Orchestra. His "Parade of the ANZACs" was played at Gallipoli and on the Western Front.

Launceston had a rather unsettled beginning. Matthew Flinders and Tom Bass explored and named the Tamar River estuary in 1798 as part of their circumnavigation of Tasmania which proved that it was an island.

By the beginning of the 19th century, the Government in Sydney was becoming anxious about the intentions of the French in Australia, so Governor King in 1804 sent Lieutenant Colonel William Paterson to establish a settlement on the north coast of Tasmania.

The settlement on the east bank of the estuary was named George Town, but did not last long. An inadequate water supply forced the settlers to move across the estuary to a new settlement named York Town. After less than a year, in 1805, the settlement was moved to the head of the Tamar where Launceston, at first named Patersonia, now stands.

Launceston slowly became the major port of northern Tasmania. Wharves and warehouses lined the river banks and a grand Customs House, still standing, was built in 1855. Flour mills and textile mills were built to serve the surrounding areas.

The discovery of minerals—tin at Mount Bischoff in 1871, gold and copper at Mount Lyell in 1881, silver at Zeehan in 1882—gave the north of the island and Launceston a 'golden age of prosperity'. Farming land was also opening up and the region started producing potatoes, fruit, cheese and butter.

In 1914, Premier A.G. Ogilvie had the foresight to initiate planning to build hydroelectric plants on the central plateau. By the 1960s, Tasmania's generating capacity was attracting such industries as the Bell Bay aluminium smelters. A consequence of the flooding of Lake Pedder in the 1970s for hydro power generation was the beginning of the environmental movement in Australia.

The export of processed metals is one of the main activities bringing money into Tasmania—the other being tourism. Because economic growth slowed, Georgian and Victorian buildings in Hobart and Launceston remain untouched and are now a great tourist drawcard. The green and gentle landscapes of eastern Tasmania and the West Coast wilderness areas attract thousands of visitors every year. Launceston is one of the main destinations. A stroll through City Park with its venerable trees, magnificent drinking fountain and picturesque Lithgow Rotunda is an opportunity to feel part of Launceston's past.

IN MEMORY OF
ALEX. F. LITHGOW
BANDMASTER ORCHESTRAL
LEADER AND COMPOSER
LAUNCESTON 1894-1929
ERECTED BY
HIS OLD COMRADES AND FRIENDS

cataract gorge
launceston, tasmania

Cataract Gorge in the heart of Launceston has long been admired for its dramatic landscape. William Collins, exploring in 1804, thought it "the most beautiful scenery in the world". The cliffs and cataracts, forest and ferns later appealed to the Victorian aesthetic, and moves to make it accessible to the citizens of Launceston began early.

William Barnes arrived in Van Diemen's Land in 1824 and settled in Launceston. He was granted 400 hectares on the South Esk River. He leased 12 hectares of this land at a peppercorn rental to the City and Suburbs Improvement Association to build a path on the north bank of the South Esk River from its confluence with the Tamar to the First Basin. His descendants gave more land for the Cataract Gorge Reserve. The 192 hectare reserve includes several natural habitats—grasslands, dry and wet forests—providing sanctuaries for wildlife.

Already featuring in tourist guides in the 1870s, the Gorge by 1890 was being developed into a pleasure ground. At the end of the path on the north bank, visitors would find the picnic ground and the rotunda, surrounded by exotic trees and rhododendrons and decorated with wandering peacocks.

The rotunda was built in 1896 as a "music pavilion" presented by the ladies of Launceston to the Cataract Cliff Grounds. This was the second rotunda in the

reserve, the first having been so close to the river that the sounds of the cataract interfered with the band music. The new rotunda was designed by Harry Norton Taylor, Superintendant of Works and Honorary Engineer for the City and Suburbs Improvement Association. The plaque on the rotunda reads:

This Music Pavilion was created by a committee of the Ladies of Launceston and presented to the Cataract Cliff Grounds AD1896—Mrs N H Taylor Hon Treas; Mrs W Sorell Hon Sec; N H Taylor Hon Archt.

I assume Mrs Taylor was the wife of the pavilion's designer.

The Music Pavilion—a very appropriate and attractive name—is a timber framed structure on a masonry base. Paired timber columns support a curved sheet metal roof topped with an onion dome and finial. A solid balustrade and a pierced timber frieze complete the design.

Further up the Gorge at Duck Reach, Launceston Council built a turbine driven power station and, on 10 December 1895, Launceston became the first town in the Southern Hemisphere to switch to electric power. The power station was decommissioned in 1955 and is now the Interpretive Centre. Later additions were the suspension bridge at the head of the First Basin in 1940 and the chair lift from the Cliff Grounds and its restaurant to the main car park, cafe, pool and grassed picnic area in 1972. River cruises start from the city and go part-way up the Gorge as far as the first cataract, sailing under the handsome Kings Bridge which was constructed in Manchester, shipped out and erected in 1864.

The cottage perched on the path adjacent to Kings Bridge was built in the 1890s for the gatekeeper of the Cliff Grounds and is now used for the Artists in Residence program.

Cataract Gorge Reserve is still a favourite place for the people of Launceston. Symphony in the Park and many other events are held there. Illuminated at night, it retains the feeling of the exotic and dramatic that entranced William Collins over two hundred years ago.

elder park
adelaide

To see the most beautiful band rotunda in Australia, you must go to Adelaide. In Elder Park on the banks of the Torrens River is a delicate cast iron bandstand, one of only two fully imported bandstands from the Macfarlane's Saracen Foundry in Glasgow.

When a weir was built across the Torrens in 1881, the Mayor T.E. Smith thought the banks of the newly formed lake would be an ideal site for a bandstand. Three fundraising concerts did not raise enough and Sir Thomas Elder came to the rescue. Sir Thomas, born in Scotland in 1818, was a great benefactor of South Australia. He financed copper mines, built up a vast pastoral empire and founded, with others, the wool broking firm Elder Smith.

While on a visit to Scotland, Sir Thomas wrote to Mayor Smith, saying that he had "taken the liberty" of ordering a bandstand from McFarlane's. The design, one of their grandest, is featured in the sixth edition of their catalogue. Sir Thomas also paid for its shipping to Adelaide and £100 towards its erection in August 1882. The opening by Mayor Smith in front of 2,000 guests was accompanied by a specially commissioned piece of music entitled "The Rotunda March" performed by the Adelaide City Brass Band.

The city now had a special rotunda that reflected the citizens' self esteem—the people of Adelaide and South Australia considered themselves a cut above the East Coast colonists whose beginnings lay in the convict era. The colony of South Australia was the product of the change of thought on methods of colonisation being discussed in England. New moral thought was that colonies should be planned and ways developed to allow suitable emigrants to work and eventually own land in the new colony.

The person who put these ideas into a practical form was Edward Gibbon Wakefield. He had plenty of time to formulate his thoughts in 1830 while in gaol in London (for abducting an underage heiress), where he anonymously wrote a series of "letters from Sydney" about his supposed failures as a colonist, blaming them on the "faults of the colony", even though he had never been there. Colonial Secretary Robert Gouger published the "letters" and, after several of his and Wakefield's attempts to form private companies to promote their plan, their principles were incorporated in the South Australian Colonisation Act of 1834. Crown land was to be sold to investors and those funds used to finance the free passage of suitable migrants who would be required to work for wages until they had saved enough to buy their own land.

The person chosen to survey the land in this new colony was Colonel William Light. Made Surveyor General in January 1836, Light set sail for what was a little known part of the Australian continent.

On arrival in the Gulf of St Vincent and after searching for some time, Light selected a site for the new settlement eight miles south of the entrance to a river (later named the Torrens) and proclaimed it Adelaide, after Queen Adelaide, Queen of King William I.

Divided in two by the river, his beautifully realised town plan aligned streets north-south and east-west, surrounded by parkland. It is probable that this layout was influenced by plans in a book written by a Colonel T.J. Masten in 1830. Titled *The Friend of Australia: Or a Plan for Exploring the Interior, and for Carrying on a Survey of the Whole Continent of Australia*, it shows a similar (theoretical) town plan (p.183).

Settlers began arriving even before the survey was completed in March 1837, by which time about 2,500 people had arrived and built their huts wherever they could until allocated land to work on.

Colonisation continued rapidly and before long pressure began for the colony to become self governing. In 1856, the British Government ratified a new constitution for South Australia, including a bicameral parliament with a thirty-six member House of Assembly and a Legislative Council of eighteen.

Federation in 1901 was a cause for great celebration and included a visit from the Duke and Duchess of York on 9 July 1901. By then, Adelaide was a thriving city with substantial buildings lining the wide main streets as Light had envisioned. After a half century of economic ups and downs, including two world wars, drought and depression, the state began a long period of growing prosperity assisted by a great increase in immigration. The first Adelaide Festival was held in March 1960 and the Festival has continued expanding to include a Writers Festival and a Fringe Festival. It quickly outgrew the available venues and in 1973 the Adelaide Festival Centre was built on the edge of Elder Park, the home of the glorious bandstand. At the supper after the opening of the bandstand in 1882, a committee was formed to arrange regular performances at the bandstand. Now, the regular performances are in the grand Festival Hall, but I am sure that the citizens of Victorian Adelaide would approve. The imposing bandstand, its delicate and ornate cast iron painted in brilliant colours and adorned with gilded details, is a fitting counterpoint to the massive sculptural Festival Centre.

As *The Adelaide Observer* commented at its opening in 1882: "The rotunda, which is a splendid piece of iron-work, is a gift which the citizens cannot too highly appreciate, and it will be a most prominent ornament to the city." ❖

strathalbyn
south australia

The Angas River makes a gentle loop around the Soldiers' Memorial Gardens, the attractive setting for Strathalbyn's bandstand. The early settlers who had the forethought to make the peninsula the centre of their town plan were Scots who arrived in South Australia in 1839.

The Rankine brothers John, William and James and Colonel James Dawson were the first to settle the district and by 1840 *The Adelaide Chronicle* of 26 August was commenting that "the Angas or Strathalbyn district is now becoming very thickly settled, is indeed, we believe, almost the best stocked survey in the province".

This early prosperity is reflected in the quality of the buildings in Strathalbyn. St Andrew's Church, a handsome structure in a prominent setting behind the gardens, was begun in 1844 and the town's other stone buildings make streetscapes worthy of the town's heritage listing.

The peninsula was used for grazing cattle for many years, but by 1868 Joseph Elliot, the owner and editor of *The Southern Argus* newspaper, was making a plea for the "beautification" of the peninsula thus: "The meandering course of the river with its curved and graceful outlines ... might be rendered full of scenic effect."

By 1871, some planting had been done, fenced off from the cattle which wandered down a cart track to the ford. But it was not until 1901 that Joseph Elliot's granddaughter, Emmie, supported by her father J.W.E. Elliot, the new publisher of *The Southern Argus*, gathered sufficient funds to erect a flagpole and fence the reserve to exclude the wandering cattle altogether.

On 2 March 1905, J.W.E. Elliot published an interview with Dr David Fleming of the splendidly named Microscopical Section of the Royal Society. In it, Dr Fleming made comments on the state of the reserve and offered suggestions for tree planting. These remarks inspired Mayor Edward Jones Tucker to call a public meeting in April to consider beautifying the peninsula and forming a Town Improvement Committee. He suggested a bandstand be built—and he just happened to have a set of drawings with him. The design was by local builder and undertaker Alexander Caldwell.

Elliot chaired the public appeal launched to raise funds for its construction. The recently formed brass band approached the Council for funding for the bandstand, but the Council "could not see its way clear to accede to the request of the band". However, J.W.E. and Emmie managed to collect £60 and the band supplemented that. Together they raised £118.

Calwell's tender was accepted and building began in December 1912. The octagonal bandstand 20 feet (6 metres) in diameter has an ogee-shaped metal roof supported on cast iron columns cast in the Hartley Foundry in Port Adelaide.

The Southern Argus on 27 February 1913 reported that the colour scheme was "chocolate relieved by delicate green ironwork and scotias picked out in 'old gold'". At the grand opening, J.W.E. Elliot was given credit for starting the project. The band, under the leadership of W.J. Wallis, played a selection of pieces.

In January 1919, a public meeting was called to consider how to remember the World War dead, thirty-three from the town and thirty-one from the surrounding districts. The memorial with sculpture by Douglas Richardson was unveiled by the Governor, Sir Lancelot Stirling, on 14 August 1919 and the park was named the Soldiers' Memorial Gardens.

Another addition to the gardens was the aptly named Children's Bridge, a concrete footbridge from the end of the peninsula to Commercial Road. Erected in 1919, it was the gift of Mr William Richardson as a memorial to his wife. At the opening of the bridge on 11 December, *The Southern Argus* reported that there was "a procession of pioneers ... a number of old ladies and then a procession of close on 300 school children [who] wended their way over the structure, round the rotunda and back, then to the flat near the school where they were sumptuously regaled ... Before the general public crossed over, the very youngest member of the community, a baby born a couple of hours earlier was carried over the structure, both ends of the ladder of life being thus represented by the crossers of the bridge."

Strathalbyn continued to prosper quietly between the two world wars. The new high school opened in 1927 and the reservoir was completed in 1935. As well as working hard, people had time to play tennis, go on picnics, play croquet and polo and go to band concerts given in the rotunda. There were twenty bandsmen in a 1933 photograph, showing that music was important to the townspeople.

Today, Strathalbyn with its heritage-listed buildings, many filled with shops selling antiques and "collectibles", and set in a gentle landscape of rolling hills and stone walls, has become a popular tourist destination. The Soldiers' Memorial Garden and the bandstand with St Andrew's Church in the background is the serene centre of this attractive town.

mannum
south australia

On the banks of the lower Murray River in the town of Mannum, a rotunda in the Mary Ann Reserve stands to the memory of William Richard Randell. Those two names are linked in commemoration of an extraordinary period of invention and adventure on Australia's greatest river.

The Murray and its tributaries have a catchment area covering almost one-fifth of the continent. First discovered by the explorers Hume and Howell, it was later explored more thoroughly by Charles Sturt who named it after the Secretary of State for the Colonies, Sir George Murray.

While South Australia's Governor Gawler (1838–41) spoke of the River as a useful waterway to move the produce of inland areas, it was left to Governor Young (1847–54) to encourage the South Australian Government to take positive action to open up the river to trade. The outcome was a "bonus" of £4000 offered in 1850 by the Government "to be equally divided between the first two iron steamers of not less than 40 horsepower ... which successfully navigate the Murray from Goolwa to at least the junction of the Darling". The steamers had to be assembled on the River.

Two people took up the challenge. One was William Richard Randell, the son of William Beavis Randell who owned a flour mill at Gumeracha, west of the future Mannum. William Beavis leased government riverfront land in 1851 with the view of taking his flour and other supplies to the station holders up the river.

When son William heard of the bonus, he and his brother Thomas George and a carpenter decided to build a steamer in answer to the challenge. William had never seen a river steamer, but had experience of steam engines. They built a sturdy timber craft and a Mr Ghelkin, an Adelaide engineer, supplied the massive boiler which can still be seen in the local museum. The steamer, named the *Mary Ann* after their mother, was 55 feet (16.5 metres) long and cost £800. On 4 March 1853, the Randell brothers took their new craft with 20 tons of cargo upriver on a trial run. The river was low and they had to return after being stuck on a sandbank west of Renmark. After some modifications, they were ready to enter the great riverboat race.

The other contender was Captain Francis Cadell, a very different person from the quiet, religious William Randell. Cadell was a flamboyant and experienced sea captain whose steamer *Lady Augusta*—prudently named after the wife of the Governor—was built in Sydney. She was much larger than the *Mary Ann*: 105 feet (31.5 metres) long and with two engines. Cadell crossed the river mouth in *Lady Augusta* on 16 August 1853 and set off up the river from Goolwa on 25 August.

Unbeknownst to Cadell, the Randells had already left in the little *Mary Ann* on 15 August. The *Lady Augusta* caught up with them during the night of 14 September. While the Randells slept peacefully on the river bank, the *Lady Augusta* passed them with a great clamour. Over the next few days, they passed each other several times.

Ultimately, the *Lady Augusta* won, arriving at Swan Hill at 3 p.m. on 17 September, two hours ahead of the *Mary Ann*. Neither received a share of the £4,000, as neither fulfilled the conditions of the bonus—the *Mary Ann* not being built of iron and the *Lady Augusta* not having been built on the river.

River traffic boomed. By 1867, there were at least thirty steamers, carrying all sorts of goods to the settlers—soap and saddles, windows and tombstones—and returning with loads of wool and wheat. One boat, the *Emily Jane,* carried a team of dressmakers who took orders on the way upriver and delivered the finished clothing on the way back. Many of the streamers were built or maintained at Mannum and the town grew rapidly to service the river trade. In the 1860–70 decade, nearly 20,000 bales of wool were unloaded at Mannum for overland transport to Adelaide.

John and David Shearer started a blacksmithing business in 1876, repairing steamers and farmers' implements, and shoeing horses. John Shearer also built a steam car with a differential which achieved a speed of 15 miles per hour (24 km/h). He then turned his attention to the design and manufacture of farm machinery. This business grew rapidly and the Shearers built a wharf to distribute their machinery up the river. The factory, now owned by Horwood Bagshaw, still manufactures farm machinery.

Captain Johan Georg Arnold (known as George) arrived in Mannum in 1899 and at first worked with the Randells at the dry dock they had built. He bought the dry dock in 1913 and became a ship owner and builder. He was a good employer and benefactor to the town.

River traffic on the upper Murray started to decline in the 1890s when both New South Wales and Victoria built country rail lines; however, it continued at lower volume until the 1940s with cargoes of wool from the Darling. The *Marion*, a paddle wheeler built in 1897 continued in the trade until 1950 and, now restored, takes tourists out from Mannum on short day cruises.

William Randell died in 1911 and the local people erected the memorial rotunda in 1913 in the Mary Ann Reserve with the great river its backdrop. Built by Burt Dahl, it survived until a very large tree fell on it on 18 February 1989. It was rebuilt by Leon Warhurst. Cast iron columns, brackets and frieze support its corrugated ogee-shaped metal roof topped by a sheet metal spire.

Mannum is now a thriving tourist centre with house boats for hire and river cruises. Now and then, the majestic paddle steamer *Murray Princess* comes around the bend with tourists who have had a glimpse of life on the river. They come ashore at the Mary Anne Reserve and walk past the rotunda dedicated to William Richard Randell, the builder of the first steam boat on the Murray. ❖

market square
burra, south australia

Burra's rotunda sits in a commanding position in the town's market square. The square is surrounded by the substantial buildings of an established country town, but its history as a tough mining settlement is quite different.

Less than ten years after Adelaide was founded, copper was discovered near Burra Burra Creek in 1845. The South Australian Mining Association won the race to buy the lucrative site from the colonial government.

By 1851, the town called Kooringa which sprang up was the second largest in South Australia and its "monster mine" was producing the high grade copper which helped the struggling colony of South Australia out of debt. From 1847 to 1864, annual returns to investors never fell below to 200% of their investment and for fourteen of those years were 300% or better, reaching an astonishing 800% in 1850.

This largesse did not benefit the mine workers. They had to pay 6 pence a bucket for fresh water which was at a great premium in the sweltering summer months. They even had to pay to have their picks sharpened. Another instance of the company's fixation on profit was the addendum attached to the grant of land to the Church of England to build a church: if payable copper was found under the church, the company reserved the right to knock it down.

The Ladies' Cheer Up Band with the Navy, Navy Day 1917.

The company had built houses for its workers, but the miners, mostly Cornishmen and staunch individualists, were not willing to pay the exorbitant rents demanded by the owners and instead dug homes out of the high banks of the Burra Burra Creek. The few advantages of these "houses" were that they cost nothing and were cool in summer and warm in winter—the disadvantages were the unhygienic conditions, the threat of flooding and the risk of nasty things being dropped down the chimney into the cooking pot from the bank above. Eventually, three major floods in 1851 caused the company to insist that they be abandoned, but two that have been restored give visitors a vivid impression of what life was like in the dugouts.

By 1863, the ore was becoming difficult to obtain and the price of copper was dropping: finally, in 1867, underground mining ceased and the company converted to open cut mining, the first in Australia. This proved unsuccessful and mining operations ceased on 29 September 1877, the miners being given a week's pay in lieu of notice. Various companies later tried reopening the mine, achieving little, until 1916 when mining ceased. From then on, except for eleven years when an open cut mine operated briefly from 1970 to 1981, Burra was left as solely a centre for agricultural and pastoral pursuits. Since the 1960s, tourism has added an important element to Burra's economy.

Burra became the centre for the surrounding farming land, helped by an 1869 act of Parliament permitting up to 640 acres (260 hectares) to be bought on credit, attracting to the district farmers who successfully grew wheat and bred high quality Merino sheep. The town grew slowly; the railway arrived in 1870 and the imposing Burra Model School was opened.

The market square was the focus of the town's activities. A public pump and trough were installed in 1881. The beautiful new bandstand was built between November 1910 and January 1911 and the opening ceremony was held on 1 February 1911. The plaque over the entrance reads: "Erected by the inhabitants of the town and district of Burra in memory of our beloved King Edward VII. John McLaren, Mayor, January, 1911". It is an excellent example of cast iron design, cast and built by James Robinson's Britannia Foundry in Gawler. The delicate cast iron columns and frieze are complemented by the double curve of the corrugated iron roof. The ball and weather vane complete a very pleasing building.

In February 1917, in patriotic response to the emotional needs of soldiers returning from the First World War, ladies of Burra formed the Burra Ladies Cheer-up Band. This remarkable band was an offshoot of another remarkable group of women: the Cheer-up Society formed by Alexandrina Seager in November 1914 at the beginning of the Great War, when the First AIF was about to embark. Visiting her son in a pre-embarkation camp, she saw the emotional needs of many young men, mostly mere boys, anxiously waiting to depart to an uncertain fate. She set her new society to the task of entertaining them and, as the name describes, providing cheery comfort. The society was unique to South Australia and had eighty country branches, including Burra. Mrs Seager also inaugurated Violet Day, a day of remembrance in South Australia.

By 1917, the war was in its third year with no end in sight and Australians at home were seeing more and more its horrific consequences in the wounded, maimed and war weary men now returning home, boys no more, in need of comfort above all. The Burra Ladies Cheer-up Band responded to this need. It was in constant demand, playing in country towns and Adelaide and by May 1919 had played on many occasions greeting returned soldiers at the Burra railway station. In a report in 1920, Mayor Mr E. Crewes said he had been "about 165 times to welcome boys back at the station, but the Ladies Band had done more".

With the Ladies Cheer-up Band providing the music, a memorial service on Violet Day, 4 July 1919, was held at the rotunda which was decorated with wreaths from the families and friends of the men who did not return—"our fallen heroes". The Ladies Cheer-Up Band welcomed its last "boys" on 10 March 1920, but stayed on to take part in the visit of the Prince of Wales to Adelaide. Its final appearance was in Adelaide on Violet Day, 11 July 1920.

The Burra Town Council bought the mine site in 1960 and opened it as a tourist feature in 1961. The mine site shows the influence of the Cornishmen who were recruited to work the mine. Two stone engine house chimneys (one of which was moved to the mine site entrance in 1971), Morphett's Engine House, built in 1858, and other stone buildings show the stone working skills of the men from Cornwall. Morphett's Engine House was restored in 1986 and houses an interpretive display of the huge Cornish beam engines once used to pump water out of the mines.

The Burra and District branch of the National Trust opened a museum in the Bon Accord Mine buildings in 1986. Restoration of many buildings, including Paxton Square, a complex of 33 miners' cottages, was completed and the cottages can now be rented for a very comfortable stay.

The Australian national committee of ICOMOS (International Council on Monuments and Sites) met in Burra in 1979 and developed a charter for practical ways to assess and care for places of cultural significance. This charter has now been adopted worldwide and is known as the Burra Charter.

Burra was proclaimed a State Heritage Area in 1993—a fitting designation for a town of great significance to South Australia. ❖

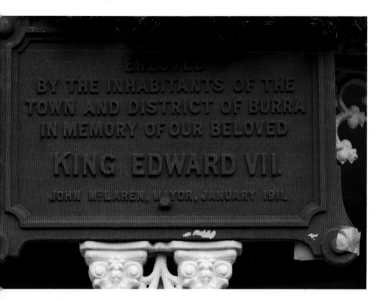

kings park
perth

M ount Eliza, the site of Kings Park, has always been a significant place, known as Kaarta Gar-up by the Nyoongar people. The permanent spring at the foot of the escarpment has always sustained life in that dry landscape.

The first European known to have landed in the Swan River area was Willem de Vlaming, a captain of the Dutch East India Company, who was sent to search for survivors from one of the Company's ships believed to have been wrecked on the West Coast. Anchoring at Rottnest Island on 11 January 1697, where he mistook the quokkas for rats, he explored a little way up the Swan River where, much to his astonishment, he found black swans. He also noted Mt Eliza and its spring.

Captain James Stirling was a distinguished naval officer who, like many, found himself ashore on half pay at the end of the Napoleonic Wars. His fortunes changed in 1826 when the British Government, concerned about French intentions in the Pacific and Australia, gave him command of the new *HMS Success* and ordered him to New South Wales to move the garrison on Melville Island to a more suitable place.

While waiting in Sydney for the end of the monsoon season, Stirling convinced Darling that the recent French presence in southern Australian waters should be countered by establishing a British presence on the west coast of the continent. Governor Darling agreed and Stirling set sail in March 1827, arriving at the mouth of

she was obviously a woman of spirit. A foundation stone was to be laid at the spot where Barrack Street is today. Unfortunately, no suitable stone could be found, so the resourceful Mrs Dance cut down a tree (or helped cut it down) and volleys, speeches and cheers completed the ceremony. The name Perth was chosen by Captain Stirling, in keeping with the wishes of Sir George Murray, the Secretary for the Colonies, who was a family friend and whose home was in Perth, Scotland.

The need to get a land grant before the end of 1830 caused an armada of ships to sail for Perth. By 1831, 1 million acres had been allocated, but very few were under cultivation. Life in the colony was a struggle with the shortage of food being the most pressing need. With little labour and financial resources, progress was slow, and eventually the British government gave in and ticket-of-leave male convicts began arriving in 1850. They built roads, public buildings and other improvements, but when convict transportation to Australia ceased in 1868, the colony was still in difficulties.

This changed with extraordinary rapidity after gold was discovered in Western Australia in 1886. Hopeful prospectors poured in and the major discoveries at Coolgardie in 1892 and Kalgoorlie in 1893 put the colony on a firm economic footing. Sir John Forrest and C.Y. O'Connor blasted the reef at the entrance to Fremantle Harbour and Perth became one of the world's busiest gold ports.

The site of Kings Park was named Mt Eliza by Sir James Stirling after the wife of Governor Darling. Surveyor General John Septimus Roe recognised that it was a special place and said it was to be set aside for public use; however, by 1835, it was being logged and timber felling continued until 1871 when Roe's successor had 1.75 square miles (2.6 square kilometres) set aside as a public reserve.

Sir John Forrest had the area enlarged in 1890 when he was president of the first Board appointed under the *Parks and Reserves Act*. Perth Park was opened in August 1895. The name was changed to King's Park in 1901 to mark the accession of Edward VII. The park has developed and today you can visit the Botanic Garden with its displays of Western Australian wildflowers, and the Western Australian War Memorial, and walk among the tree tops on the Lottery West Federation Walkway. Two thirds of the park is still in its bushland state.

In 1897, the first of two rotundas in the park was built. Designed by Perth architect, Archer William Hoskings, the timber framed building has timber brackets, friezes and a tiled roof. Further along the escarpment with a similar spectacular view is a second rotunda built in 1900 with similar timber detailing and tiled roof, also designed by Hoskings. Both are extremely popular for weddings—a romantic place to tie the knot, with the city, the river and the ocean as a backdrop in one of Australia's most extensive and beautiful parks.

the Swan River two weeks later. Sailing up-river, he admired the "rich and romantic" landscape.

Returning to Sydney, Stirling urged Darling to establish a west coast colony. Darling agreed, but the suggestion fell on deaf ears in London. Eventually, after more persuasive argument from Stirling and more alarming rumours about French activities, the government in London decided to support the idea of a Swan River colony on two conditions:

1. On no account was it to be a penal colony;
2. The government would give only minimal assistance.

In addition, free land grants were to be made to all settlers who arrived before the end of 1830.

Captain James Howe Fremantle in *HMS Challenger* accompanied by the store ship *HMS Sulphur* with soldiers of the 63rd Regiment aboard arrived at the Swan River on 2 May 1829. On 17 June Captain Irwin of the 63rd read the proclamation of the Colony of Western Australia.

On 12 August, the King's birthday, the official party rowed up the Swan River. In the party was Helen Barbara Dance, wife of Commander Dance of the *Sulphur*;

albany
western australia

Albany lies on the shores of beautiful Princess Royal Harbour in King George Sound on the south coast of Western Australia and is a favourite destination for visitors and retirees.

It was very different for 30,000 Australians and New Zealanders who assembled there in October 1914—the Australian Imperial Force (AIF) and the New Zealand Expeditionary Force (NZEF), jointly later dubbed the ANZACs while in Egypt before the Gallipoli landings. They left on 1 November in 28 Australian and six New Zealand troopships protected by six warships. Sadly, the sights of the beautiful harbour and sound were the last that very many saw of Australia. A good vantage point to wave them goodbye would have been the Queen Victoria Jubilee bandstand on Stirling Terrace, on the clifftop above the harbour.

The bandstand originated in a proposal of the Mayor, J. Moir, in 1890 that the embankment between Stirling Terrace and the foreshore be improved in time for the Diamond Jubilee of Queen Victoria. One improvement he proposed was a bandstand overlooking new gardens to be known as Queen's Park. Partly funded by a state government grant of £150, a Council contribution of £90 and public subscriptions, the bandstand was built by a local carpenter and joiner, Nobby Clark, to the design of Robert Greenshields. Mayor Moir, who performed the opening ceremony on 23

May 1898, remarked that he "hoped it would be the means of giving entertainment with the assistance of the band and was sure the townspeople and visitors would appreciate it"—and they still do.

The timber framed building is an unusual shape—it has a pitched metal clad roof over timber columns and a timber handrail and balustrade; while the landward side is straight and aligned with the street edge, the harbour side projects over the cliff with curved ends on a stone base. The original gabled entrance porch was removed in the 1940s when the road was widened.

On top of Mount Clarence, one of the two dramatic hills that embrace the town, is a heart stirring memorial to those who did not return. It was originally erected in Port Said, in 1932 in memory of the Australian and New Zealand soldiers killed in the Sinai and Palestine campaigns of the First World War. After suffering major damage during the Suez Crisis in 1956, the base and the remaining parts of the metal casting were brought to Australia in 1959. The two figures, an Australian and a New Zealand soldier with their two horses, were recast in Australia and the memorial was rededicated by Prime Minister Sir Robert Menzies on 11 October 1964.

King George Sound had been named after King George III by Captain George Vancouver RN, who spent some time there in September 1791, remarking that it was a "capacious port". He was one of several explorers who visited in the 18th and 19th centuries.

Matthew Flinders, that meticulous explorer, put into King George Sound in December 1801 to have *Investigator* repaired. He stayed a month, surveying and making astronomical observations, while Robert Brown, the botanist, collected 500 species of plants, 300 of which were previously unknown. The local Aborigines were cautious, but friendly, and liked their gifts—most popular were handkerchiefs and red night caps. Flinders had his fifteen Marines execute a musket drill for them before they left and it impressed all who watched.

The French also explored along the coast—D'Entrecasteaux in 1792; Nicholas Baudin in 1802–03 with three ships, *Naturaliste*, *Casuarina* and *Geographe*; then Dumont d'Urville in *Astrolabe* in 1826. Governor Darling in Sydney was anxious about French intentions in the area and decided in 1826 to establish a military outpost in King George Sound. Major Edmund Lockyer was sent with a party of soldiers and convicts in the brig *Amity* to establish a strategic outpost to signify that British possession extended over the whole continent of Australia. They arrived on Christmas Day 1826 after an appalling seven week voyage. On 21 January 1827, Lockyer proclaimed the western part of the continent a British possession, naming the settlement Fredericktown after Frederick, Duke of York and Albany. They celebrated by issuing extra flour, suet and raisins for a pudding, with a seine net's catch of fish for the local Aborigines.

Sealers and whalers had for some years established camps on islands in the Sound. They came from many countries—most were American and all were an unruly, unpleasant lot. When Major Lockyer heard that one group had abducted some of the local women, he sent a patrol to rescue the women, return them to their tribe, and arrest the kidnappers to face justice later in Sydney.

The troops and convicts were recalled to Sydney in 1831. Dr Alexander Collie was appointed the first Government Resident in April 1831, after Fredericktown

was placed under the control of the Swan River Colony (later Perth) under Governor Stirling who changed its name to Albany.

A whaling station was established in 1833 and supplying whaling ships became an important part of the local economy. By the middle of the 19th century, Albany became the first port of call for mail ships from Britain and remained so until the port of Fremantle was opened up in 1897.

Thereafter, Albany was a timber, agricultural and whaling town. Whaling was a major industry after the Second World War. The Albany Whaling Company, established in 1947, lasted only three years. Cheyne's Beach Whaling Company at Frenchman's Bay was more successful, operating from 1952 until 1978 when whaling ceased. Today the site is a whaling museum and whales have returned to the Sound.

Henry Lawson visited Albany in 1890 and described it: "Albany will never change much. It is a pretty town, but vague. It seems to exist in a some-where-on-the-horizon sort of way. I like it all the better for that." Albany is certainly not vague today, but it is still pretty and many people choose to visit or live there and enjoy its pleasant climate, white sand beaches, turquoise bays and contrasting wild coastline—and one of the best vantage points is the Queen Victoria Jubilee bandstand that has been so much a part of Albany's past. ❖

kalgoorlie
western australia

You have to travel nearly 600 kilometres east of Perth to see one of Australia's outstanding bandstands. There it sits in splendour in Hammond Park; an octagonal timber pavilion with a surrounding wide verandah, essential in Kalgoorlie's fierce climate, the whole surmounted by an onion dome topped by a crescent. Originally in Victoria Park in the centre of Kalgoorlie, it was a cool refuge for the hot and dusty citizens. Everybody went to Victoria Park for family picnics on Boxing Day to sit in the shade, look at the birds and animals in the little zoo and listen to the band strike up in the bandstand.

Author Mollie Dinham, who grew up in Kalgoorlie, describes in *Travels to Exotic Places* the excitement of going to the park in the period after the First World War: "As children we looked forward to the Sunday afternoon picnics in this exotic paradise ... from the heat and dust of the day, we passed through wrought iron gates into a magical area, into a Secret Garden." (p.212)

The heat and dust were in the forefront of the minds of the prospectors who fought their way here, lured by talks of gold. Gold had been found at Coolgardie in 1892 and prospectors fanned out over the surrounding areas looking for new finds. A rumour that there was gold at Mt Yule 60 km away to the east decided Paddy Hannan and his mates, Dan O'Shea and Thomas Flanagan, to join a group headed there. They waited in a spot in a valley that later became Kalgoorlie for the water wagon to catch up with them, and Hannan and his mates whiled away the time by doing some prospecting—with astonishing results. Using the excuse of a lost horse, they stayed behind the main group, staked their claim and recovered gold, gold, gold. Hannan jumped on his horse and raced back to Coolgardie to pay his licence fee—and the rush was on.

Within weeks the site was covered with mining leases, the scrub vanished and the valley became a dust bowl. Albert Gaston in his memoir *Coolgardie Gold* tells of how he wore his only shirt inside out on Sundays to look a little cleaner than his usual red ochre colour. Hot on the heels of the prospectors came the camel teams and wagons with water, food, clothing, boots, cases of whiskey, barrels of beer and timber for gold shakers.

While prospectors were "dry blowing" to find gold at Hannan's, a small syndicate in Perth sent two of its members, Sam Pearce and William Brookman, in June 1893 to peg out many leases on some low ironstone hills south of Hannan's. First known facetiously as "Brookman's Sheep Run", the hills were found to contain enormous quantities of gold—a golden fleece for Brookman's sheep! The field became known as the Golden Mile.

Money poured into Kalgoorlie when news of the wealth of the Golden Mile reached London. Symbolising this flood of riches and the self confidence it generated was the construction of the handsome buildings which still give Hannan Street, Kalgoorlie's main street, its grand appearance. The post office and government offices built in 1900, the Town Hall built in 1908 for the huge sum of £40,000, and the

many ornate hotels give the visitor a glimpse of the vitality of Kalgoorlie in the boom days before the First World War.

The town of Boulder grew up on the edge of the Golden Mile—not as grand as Kalgoorlie, but home to most of the miners. Now the towns have merged into Kalgoorlie-Boulder.

Victoria Park was established in 1901 and the bandstand built in 1903. A plaque in the park credits the Municipality of Kalgoorlie with the commissioning of the bandstand and its erection in three months by Edward Sears for £279 10 shillings. It was officially opened by Mayor Norbert Keenan on 5 November 1903 and from 1904 onwards on Sundays the Kalgoorlie Brass Band held well attended concerts.

Mollie Dinham remembers her father and his older sister telling her that her grandfather, Samuel Perkins, the manager of the Hannan's Central Goldmine, was the benefactor who paid for the building of the bandstand. This, she said, was stated on a brass plaque which disappeared during the Depression.

The octagonal bandstand is constructed with timber columns and arched brackets with timber infills. The surrounding timber framed verandah has cast iron brackets and a continuous cast iron frieze. The onion dome sits on a pierced metal base. The novelty of the design has raised a good deal of discussion. Some people suggest that the onion dome and the crescent on the centre pole are references to the important part played by the Afghan cameleers in the development of Kalgoorlie, but its origin remains unknown.

Kalgoorlie's boom days came to an end with the First World War. Overseas capital dried up and many miners joined up. By 1920, gold production was down to one third of its peak during the boom. Inspired by a Federal Government Gold Bonus, production grew during the Depression, but the Second World War once again brought decline. There was a brief revival after the war, but by 1976 production had fallen to one-tenth of the boom days.

Then along came entrepreneur Alan Bond who in the 1980s saw the potential for an open cut mine on the Golden Mile which was a jigsaw of mining leases. Bond did not manage to buy all the pieces of the jigsaw and the site ultimately was taken over by the Kalgoorlie Consolidated Gold Mines.

The resultant Super Pit is approximately 3.6 km long, 1.6 km wide and 500 metres deep and operates 24 hours a day. When the gold is exhausted in a few years, the Super Pit will be allowed to fill with water to become the Big Lake which Alan Bond foresaw: "We'll mine it for a hundred years and when we are finished Kalgoorlie could be the greatest resort town in WA because the pit will become a massive lake where you can sail yachts. That's how big this will be when we're finished. It will be fantastic."

Kalgoorlie has always had its share of dreamers and entrepreneurs—who knows what the future will bring for the town which has enriched Australia with its gold bonanza?

cue
western australia

By the late 1880s, gold prospectors from the eastern states were turning their attention to Western Australia, following in the wake of pastoralists who established runs on the dry inland plains.

Two of these prospectors, Bagley and Taylor, found gold around Lake Annean, southwest of the modern town of Meekatharra. The small settlement of Nannine that grew up on the lake shore was the first town of what became known as the Murchison goldfields.

Mick Fitzgerald, Edward Heffernan and Tom Cue followed the prospectors' route in 1892 and eventually found gold 80 km south of Nannine. Tom Cue rode to Nannine to report the find and that night 150 men took off for the place that later took his name. A tent town sprang up on the creek which eventually became Austin Street, Cue's main street.

Alluvial gold was found at "The Patch" to the north of Cue and a quartz reef, "The Pearling Ground", to the north-east. Company run underground mines soon followed. One mine, "The Light of Asia", operated till 1933.

Edward Heffernan looked a little further afield after his alluvial gold ran out at The Patch and found a reef of blue quartz 5.6 km south of Cue which he named the Day Dawn mine. Too difficult for a single prospector to work, it was taken over by the

Dr Ramsey's hospital tent, Cue 1895.

Great Fingall Mining Company. A substantial town called Day Dawn grew up around the mine, which finally closed in 1918. Day Dawn is now a ghost town with only one abandoned stone building remaining.

Miners flooded into the area and it soon became evident that the government needed to build the essentials of a settlement—a post office, mining registry, warden's court and police station. Tenders were let in 1894 for the construction of a building in Cue to house all these functions by the builders Aitkens and Law of Perth. This handsome building of locally quarried limestone was completed in 1895.

Supplies for the growing town came by bullock wagon or camel train from Mullewa to the south. The telephone line from Mullewa was completed in 1894, not without difficulty, as the bullock teams started using the nicely cleared straight telephone line route and the poles were frequently knocked down. The local newspaper, *The Murchison Times and Day Dawn Gazette*, kept an eye on progress and announced in October 1894: "Glad tidings Tuesday night, the line is completed. Sad tidings Wednesday night, the line won't work". Cue was finally connected to the rest of the world by telephone on 12 November 1894. A railway line from Mullewa begun in March 1896 reached Cue in April 1897. It was declared open by the Premier, Sir John Forrest, who donated a

clock for the Post Office tower, and the municipal band led the celebratory procession through town.

A reliable water supply was always a problem in that arid country. Typhoid epidemics swept through the shanties and there were few medical services. The early miners of Cue relied on the Milly Soak 8 km north of town, but it soon became obvious that a well was needed in town. The Warden, still living at Nannine, contributed £20 on behalf of the government and the miners donated their labour. The pile of soil from the well was used as a platform for speechmaking.

Later, a more reliable piped water supply was obtained from Lake Nallan, 11 km north of Cue. In 1904, Council decided to build a rotunda over the old well. It commemorates the pioneers of the Murchison district and was the social centre of town with a band playing on Saturday nights. Cast iron columns, brackets and frieze support a corrugated iron roof. The foundation stone reads: "Foundation stone laid by the Mayoress Mrs J.W. Lloyd in honour of the pioneers of the Murchison. With water bag and pick they conquered an inhospitable desert and carved out happy and prosperous towns." The rotunda's balustrade has been replaced. A drinking fountain in the centre was added in 1934 in memory of S.A. Mahood, a chairman of the District Roads Board.

The population of Cue and Day Dawn had reached 10,000 by 1900, but the boom time for the "Queen of the Murchison" was short lived. Gold output began to decline in most mines and, as in other mining towns, the First World War caused an exodus of miners who never returned.

By 1933, the population of Cue was less than 500, but the town received a boost when the Big Bell mine west of Cue was reopened by an American company in 1936. It closed from 1943 to 1945, reopened after the Second World War, and finally closed in 1954.

Today, Cue with its heritage listed buildings is a centre for the surrounding pastoral and mining industries. The rotunda standing bravely in the middle of the main street, the highway to the Pilbara mines, is a monument to the tenacious people who settled this remote country. ❖

katherine
northern territory

Katherine, "the crossroads of the North", has always been a meeting place. Groups from the Jawoyn, Dagoman and Wardaman people gathered here to harvest the plentiful seasonal food before moving on to other places. Today, Katherine, 320 kilometres south of Darwin, is at the junction of the Territory's two main highways—the Stuart and Victoria Highways.

The Stuart Highway is named after the intrepid John McDouall Stuart and Katherine derives its name from the Katherine River which was discovered and named by Stuart on 4 July 1862 after the daughter of his expedition sponsor James Chambers; her name was actually Catherine.

The Katherine Telegraph Station was established on the south bank of the Katherine River on 22 August 1872 and the telegraph extended to Darwin on 27 October. It helped open up the Northern Territory and was a vital link with the outside world for the people of the "never never". A pub and store were established near the river crossing. Mrs Aeneas Gunn describes it in *We of the Never Never*: "Coming up from the river, the Katherine settlement appeared to consist solely of the 'Pub', which, by the way, seemed to be hanging on to its own verandah post for support, we found an elongated, three-roomed building nestling under deep verandahs ... Beyond further bends in the track ... the Overland Telegraph stood on a little rise ... a tiny settlement, with a tiny permanent population of four men and two women." (p.25)

Communication improved when the railway line from Darwin reached the north side of the Katherine River in 1917. Many immigrants worked on the construction of the railway line, including a group of "White Russians", mostly from China and Manchuria, who had fought in Siberia in the Revolution of 1918–22 and emigrated to Australia between 1926 and 1928. After the completion of the railway line in 1928, many took up offers of land from the Northern Territory Administration to grow peanuts. The Russians cleared their land and struggled on for several years, eventually turning to vegetable growing which was of great importance during the Second World War when Katherine became a major military centre.

The Russians maintained their traditional Russian music and Cossack dancing and several went back to Manchuria, before returning with Russian wives. One of the most colourful men was "Galloping Jack"—Germogen Ilyich Sergeef (1900–79)—who had a hobby of creating sculptures from empty sardine cans. His most spectacular creation, "Planetarium", constructed entirely from painted cans, represents the solar system. Alone it makes a visit to the Katherine Museum worthwhile, apart from all the other interesting things displayed there.

Katherine entered another phase after the bombing of Darwin on 19 February 1942. Many facilities were moved from Darwin to Katherine which became a major staging post; the airfield was upgraded, the road to Darwin sealed, and the 120th/101st Australian General Hospital built. The airfield was bombed on 22 March 1942; eighty-four "daisy cutter" bombs were dropped on the airfield and seven on surrounding areas. One man was killed and one wounded.

Civilians started returning in 1946 and the town grew slowly, becoming a transhipping point for the cattle and agricultural industries. With the completion in 1976 of a high level bridge over the river, always prone to major floods, a reliable link was established between the Never Never and Darwin.

Nitmiluk (Katherine) Gorge was declared a National Park in 1962, gradually attracting more and more tourists to its spectacular scenery. The completion of the Ghan railway line from Adelaide to Darwin—the first train arrived in Darwin on 4 February 2004—also boosted tourist numbers.

There is plenty to see in and around Katherine, including the Gorge, Springvale homestead—the oldest in the Northern Territory—and the Katherine Museum with its informative displays on the life of Katherine. When you have done that and go outside, you can admire the elegant rotunda in the park. Built with a Bicentennial grant in 1988 from a design by Landmark Products of Strathpine, Queensland, it is a popular place for picnics, parties and weddings.

best of the rest

There are many more charming bandstands, kiosks, pavilions and rotundas throughout Australia, with their own history to explore, below are some examples for you to find.

THIS PAGE. Top left: Camperdown Park, Sydney; Bottom left: Balmoral Beach, Sydney; Top centre: Watson's Bay, Sydney; Middle centre: Robertson Park, Mudgee, NSW; Bottom centre: Queens Park, Ipswich, Queensland; Above: Edinburgh Gardens, Fitzroy, Melbourne

OPPOSITE. Top left: Lambton Park, Lambton, Newcastle, NSW; Bottom left: Botanic Gardens, Benalla, Victoria; Right: Tyrell Park, Wallsend, Newcastle, NSW

THIS PAGE. Top left: Maddingly Park, Bacchus Marsh, Victoria; Bottom left: Foreshore Reserve, Sandringham, Melbourne; Above top: King Edward Park, Newcastle, NSW; Above bottom: Queen Victoria Gardens, Melbourne

OPPOSITE. Left: Princes Park, Maryborough, Victoria; Top right: Colley Reserve, Glenelg South Australia; Bottom right: Locke Park, East Fremantle, Western Australia

list of bandstands and rotundas of Australia

There are probably other bandstands and rotundas which should be included. If you know of one, please email me at alisonrose3@bigpond.com with the date it was built, if known, and attach a photograph, if possible. This list does not include park shelters or gazebos.

I have indicated with asterisks the outstanding ones, graded * to ***.

Significance ratings
National Trust listed: NT
War Memorial: WM
State Heritage listed: HL (except in Victoria)
State Significance: SS (for Victoria only)
Regional Significance: RS (for Victoria only)

Queensland, City and Country
* Apple Tree Creek, The Reserve. 1911. HL NT
  Bowen Hills, Bowen Park. 1914. HL
*** Brisbane, New Farm Park. 1915. HL NT
** Bundaberg, Alexandra Park. 1911
*** Charters Towers, Lissner Park Kiosk. 1910. HL NT
  Cunnamulla, Main St. 2003
  Cleveland, G.J. Walker Park. Recent
  Dalby, Thomas Jack Park. Recent
  Emu Park, Bell Park. c1910. HL
  Gympie, River Rd. 1921. HL WM NT
  Ilfracombe, Main Ave. 2002. WM
** Ipswich, Queens Park. 1891. HL
  Kingaroy, Haly and William Streets. 1932. WM
  Mackay, Jubilee Park. 1935
  Mackay, Queen's Park. 1920. NT
  Maryborough, Queens Park. 1890. HL NT
  Millmerran, ANZAC Memorial Park. 1925
  Pomona, Reserve St. 1939. WM
  Sandgate, War Memorial Park. 1995. NT HL
* Shorncliffe, Moora Park. 1897. NT
** Toogoolawah, McConnel Park. 1911. NT HL
*** Townsville, The Strand. 1913. HL NT
  Wynnum, George Clayton Park. Recent

New South Wales, City
** Ashfield, Yeo Park. 1929. HL NT
*** Balmoral, The Esplanade. 1930. HL
  Balmain, Elkington Park. 1936. HL
* Burwood, Burwood Park. 1902

* Cabarita, Cabarita Park. c1903
** Cabramatta, Cabravale Memorial Park. 1919. HL WM
*** Camperdown, Hyde Park. c1888
  (Relocated to Camperdown Park 1911)
  Central Station, Belmore Park. 1910. HL
** City, Observatory Park. 1912
* Double Bay, Double Bay Park. c1892. NT
** Glebe, Dr J.H. Foley Rest Park. 1934
  Haberfield, Federation Plaza. c1988
*** Lane Cove, Lane Cove Plaza. 1983. NT
* Paddington, Moore Park. c1890. (Restored 2004)
*** Parramatta, Prince Alfred Park. 1891. NT HL
  Parramatta, Parramatta Park. 1932. HL
** Petersham, Petersham Park. 1902
* Royal Botanic Gardens, Vista Pavilion. 1907
  Ryde, Ryde Park. 1915. HL
* St Marys, Victoria Park. 1922. HL WM
* Strathfield, Strathfield Park. 1988
  Wahroonga, Wahroonga Park. 1999
** Watsons Bay, Robertson Park. 1929

New South Wales, Country
** Albury, Botanic Gardens. 1890. (Restored 1979)
*** Armidale, Central Park. 1902. NT HL
  Bangalow, Bangalow Parklands. 2016
*** Bathurst, Machattie Park. 1890. HL NT
  Blayney, Carrington Park. 1935
  Bourke, Central Park. 1898. HL
  Bowral, Corbett Gardens. 1966
  Braidwood, Ryrie Park. 1893
* Branxton, Branxton Park. 1923. HL WM
* Coolah, Queensborough Park. 1907. HL
  Cowra, Brougham Park. 1931
* Currarong, Dolphin Reserve. c1920. HL
  Deniliquin, Waring Gardens. 1913. HL
  Dubbo, Victoria Park. 1938
  Dungog. 2015. WM
** Forbes, Victoria Park. 1904. NT HL
* Ganmain, Victory Gardens. 1954
*** Glen Innes, ANZAC Park. 1912. HL
*** Goulburn, Belmore Park. 1898. NT
  Grenfell, Taylor Park. 1931. HL
  Greta, New England Highway. 1922. HL
*** Gulgong, ANZAC Park. 1918. WM
* Gundagai, Carberry Park. Unknown
  Holbrook, Ten Mile Creek Gardens. 1988

  Inverell, Campbell Park. 2005.
** Kandos, White Crescent Park. 1930. NT
  Kurri Kurri, Rotary Park, Lang St. c1928. HL WM
*** Lambton (Newcastle), Lambton Park. 1890. HL
  Leeton, Chelmsford Place. 1933
  Leeton, Community Federation Stage. 2001
** Lismore, Spinks Park. 1914. HL NT
* Lithgow, Queen Elizabeth Park. 1960. HL
  Lockhart, Walter Day Park. 2005
  Macksville, River St. 2015
*** Maitland, Maitland Park. 1908. NT
  Mayfield (Newcastle), Dangar Park. 1926
  Millthorpe, Redmond Oval. c1958. NT
** Moree, Kirkby Park. 1935. NT HL
* Moss Vale, Leighton Gardens. 1900
*** Mudgee, Robertson Park. 1903. HL NT WM
* Newcastle, Cooks Hill Park. 1993
  Newcastle, King Edward Park. 1898. HL NT
  Orange, Robertson Park. 1913. HL
** Orange, Cook Park. 1908. HL NT
  Raymond Terrace, Riverside Park. 1998
  Richmond, Richmond Park. 2002
* Shellharbour, Little Park. 1896?. HL
*** Singleton, Showgrounds. 1881. HL NT
* Tamworth, ANZAC Park. c1901
* Tenterfield, Jubilee Park. 1921
  Toronto, Regatta Park. 2001
  Tumut, Richmond Park. 1911. NT
  Wagga Wagga, University. c1890 (Relocated)
*** Wallsend (Newcastle), Tyrrell Park. 1888. NT HL WM
  Warners Bay, Riverside Park. 1998
* Wellington, Cameron Park. 1909. HL
  Windsor, McQuade Park. c1910
  Wollongong, Market Square. 1896. HL (Reproduction)
** Young, Carrington Park. 1912. HL

Australian Capital Territory
** Canberra, Glebe Park. c1983. HL NT

Victoria, Melbourne
  Canterbury, Canterbury Gardens. 1909
  Caulfield, Caulfield Park. 1921
  City, Royal Botanic Gardens, Rose Pavilion. 1897. RS
*** City, Fitzroy Gardens. 1864. NT SS
*** City, Queen Victoria Gardens. 1913. SS
  Clifton Hill, Darling Gardens. 1910

Fitzroy, Edinburgh Gardens. 1925. RS
Footscray, Railway Gardens. 1911
* Glenhuntly, Hopetoun Gardens. 1905
Greensborough, War Memorial Gardens. 1993
Kew, Alexandra Gardens. 1910
McKinnon, Joyce Park. 1990
Moonee Ponds, Maribyrnong Park. 1921. RS
Mooroolbark, Hookey Park. 1993
Mordialloc, Beach Rd. 1925. RS
Preston, Ray Bramham Gardens. 1987
* Port Melbourne, Beach Rd. 1928. SS
*** Prahran, Grattan Gardens. c1890. RS
St Kilda, Catani Gardens. 1988
** Sandringham, Foreshore Reserve. 1926. SS
* Sorrento, Point Nepean Rd. 1902
* Williamstown, Commonwealth Reserve. 1900

Victoria, Country
Alexandra, Leckie Park. c1914
Ararat, Alexandra Oval. 1924
*** Bacchus Marsh, Maddingly Park. 1906
** Bairnsdale, Main St. 1911
Ballarat, Bridge St Mall. 1981
Ballarat, Gladstone St. c1920
*** Ballarat, Sturt St, Queen Alexandra Bandstand. 1908. NT SS
*** Ballarat, Sturt St, Titanic Memorial Bandstand. 1915. NT SS
* Ballarat, Wendouree Parade. 1922
*** Beaufort, Neill St. 1903. NT SS
Beechworth, Town Hall Gardens. 1877. RS
*** Benalla, Botanic Gardens. 1911. SS
Bendigo, Hargraves Mall. 1982
Bendigo, Rosalind Park. 1995
Bentleigh, Centre Rd. 1992
Castlemaine, Botanic Gardens. 1898. (Replica)
Charlton, Elliot Park. 1926
Colac, Memorial Square. 1994
** Creswick, Albert St. 1897
Daylesford, Wombat Hill Botanic Gardens. 1993
Drouin, Civic Park. 1991
Dunolly, Gordon Gardens. 1993
Eaglehawk, Dr Catford Community Park. 1994
Ferntree Gully, Lysterfield Rd. 1984
*** Geelong, Johnstone Park. 1919. SS
** Hamilton, Botanic Gardens. c1909
*** Maryborough, Princes Park. 1905. SS NT
Merbein, Kenny Park. 1937. RS
** Mildura, Deakin Ave. 1914. SS
** Murtoa, Lake Marma Park. 1907. RS

Natimuk, Main Rd. 1921. WM
** Newstead, Newstead Gardens. 1905. RS
*** Nhill, Victoria St. 1909
Portarlington, Pier St. 1911. SS
Port Fairy, Rosebrook Rd. 1934
Queenscliff, Citizens' Park. c1907. RS
Ringwood, Staley Gardens. 1982
Rochester, Mary St. 1926
*** Rushworth, High St. 1888/1901. SS NT
Rutherglen, Rutherglen Park. 193?
** Sale, Victoria Park. 1913
Shepparton, Maude St Mall. 1990
Swan Hill, Riverside Park. 1918
Tarnagulla, Wayman St. 1886
Terang, High St. 1923. WM
Traralgon, Victory Park. 1986
*** Walhalla, Main St. 1896. HL NT
Warburton, Warburton Highway. c1904
** Warrnambool, Botanic Gardens. 1913. HL
* Woodend, Calder Highway. 1927
Yackandandah, Memorial Gardens. 1922
Yarragon, Princes Highway. 1995
Yea, High St. c1993

Tasmania
*** Launceston, City Park. 1908. HL NT
*** Launceston, Cataract Gorge. 1896. HL
*** Hobart, St David's Park. 1925. HL
* Deloraine, Deloraine Park. 1930

South Australia, Adelaide
* Adelaide Zoo, Sir Thomas Elder Rotunda. 1884. HL
*** Elder Park. 1882. HL NT
** Glenelg, Colley Reserve. 1926. HL
* Hindmarsh, Port Rd Reserve. c1920
* Kingston Gardens. 1909
Prospect, St Helens Park. c1976. HL
Unley, Soldiers' Memorial Park. 1995. (Replica)

South Australia, Country
*** Burra, Market Square. 1911. HL NT
** Clare, Soldiers Memorial Park. 1905. HL (Restored 2016)
Gawler, Pioneer Park. 2001
** Kadina, Town Square. 1897
Loxton, East Terrace. 1928. WM
** Mannum, Mary Anne Reserve. 1913
** Millicent, Memorial Gardens. 1911
Mitcham, Mitcham Reserve. 1900. WM
Mount Gambier, Vansittart Park. 1991
Peterborough, Main St. 1931. HL

Pinnaroo, Railway Terrace. 1919. WM.
** Port Augusta, Marryatt St. 1923. WM HL NT
Port Pirie, Crystal Brook. 1921
Renmark, Jarret Memorial Garden. 1931
Sedan, Sedan Park. 1935. HL
Stirling, Mt Barker Rd. Recent
*** Strathalbyn, Angas Reserve. 1913. HL NT
Tanunda, Murray St. 1980s
*** Wallaroo, Davies Square. 1897. (Relocated)

Western Australia, Perth and Fremantle
Armadale, Minnawarra Park. 1996
East Fremantle, Locke Park. 1906
*** Kings Park, Rotunda 1. 1897. NT
*** Kings Park, Rotunda 2. 1900. NT
Queen's Gardens, East Perth. Recent
Subiaco, Market Square. c1998

Western Australia, Country
*** Albany, Stirling Terrace. 1897. NT
Bindoon, Clunes Park. 2001
*** Boulder, Loop Line Park. 1903. NT
Brooklyn, Park. 2006
Bunbury, Bicentennial Square. c2001
Busselton, Mitchell Park. c1998
Coolgardie, Coolgardie Park. Recent
** Coolgardie, Tommy Talbot Park. c1897
*** Cue, Austin St. 1904. NT HL.
Dandaragan, Pioneer Memorial Park. 2005
** Denmark, The river park. 1964. HL
Dongara, Town Park. 2001
Donnybrook. Recent
* Geraldton, Lighthouse Keeper's Park. 1998
* Gingin, Granville Park. 2001
** Guildford, Stirling Square. 1998
Kalamunda, Market Square. 2000
*** Kalgoorlie, Hammond Park. 1903. NT
Kalgoorlie, St Barbara's Square. c1986
Mandurah, Eastern Foreshore Park. 1987
* Mount Barker, Keith Stephenson Park. 2012
* Narrogin, Town Park. 1923. WM
* Northam, Bernard Park, Rotunda. 1915
* Northam, Bernard Park, Sound Shell. 2011
Pingelly. 1923. WM
York, Avon Park. 1984.

Northern Territory
Katherine. 1988

bibliography

A New History of Maitland, 1983. The Council of the City of Maitland.

Albany Historical Society website.

Albany History Collection website.

Albany War Memorial website.

Alexandrina Council website.

Andrews, T., *The Singleton Index*. Singleton City Council, Singleton.

Australian Dictionary of Biography website.

Australian Dictionary of Biography, Molly Molloy.

Australian Heritage Database website.

Australian Heritage Places Inventory website.

Bailey, J., 2006, *Mr Stuart's Track*. Rand Macmillan.

Bate, W., 2003, *Luck City—The First Generation at Ballarat 1851–1901*. Melbourne University Press, Melbourne.

Bathurst City Council, 1984, Tour Book.

Blainey, G., 1971, *The Tyranny of Distance*. Sun Books, Melbourne.

Blainey, G., 1993, *The Rush That Never Ended*. Melbourne University Press, Melbourne.

Blainey, G., 1994, *A Shorter History of Australia*. William Heinemann, Australia.

Blainey, G., 2006, *A History of Victoria*. Cambridge University Press, Melbourne. Second edition, 2013.

Boyle, S., Personal correspondence.

Bray, S., Local Studies and Family History Librarian, Parramatta Heritage Centre. Personal correspondence, 2 August 2011.

Brown, J., 1980, *In Pioneer South Australia*. Rigby, Adelaide.

Buchanan, B., 2009, *Modernism Meets the Australian Bush: Harry Howard and the "Sydney Bush School" of Landscape Architecture*. PhD thesis for University of New South Wales Faculty of the Built Environment, in the National Trust Classification Report 2009.

Burke, K., 1973, *Gold and Silver—Photographs of Australian Goldfields from the Holtermann Collection*. Penguin Books, Ringwood, Victoria.

Burra History website.

Burra Record newspaper, 21 September 1877, March 1920.

Calder, M., 1977, *Early Swan River Colony*. Rigby, Perth.

Canavan, N., 1991, *The Three Towns of Katherine*. Historical Society Katherine. Revised edition, 2006.

Canavan, N., 2005, *Katherine and World War Two*. Historical Society Katherine.

Canavan, N., 2006, *The Russian Peanut Farmers 1929–1960*. Historical Society Katherine.

Carter, J., *Australian Heritage* magazine. Summer 2005 issue.

Cataract Gorge Conservation Management Plan, 2008. GHD for the Launceston City Council.

Clark, M., 1997, *Manning Clark's History of Australia*—abridged by Michael Cathcart. Melbourne University Press, Melbourne.

Colwell, M. and Naylor, A., 1981, *Adelaide—An Illustrated History*. Lansdowne Press, Melbourne.

Cooper, J.L., 1912, *The History of the City of Prahran* (revised 1924). Melbourne Printing Co., Melbourne.

Cooper, L., Personal correspondence.

Crowe, S. and S., 1972, *The Gardens of Mughul India*. Thames and Hudson, London.

Crowley, F., 1960, *Australia's Western Third—A History of Western Australia*. Heinemann, Melbourne.

Cruchley's London in 1865: A Handbook for Strangers, Showing Where to Go, How to Get There, and What to Look At. G.F. Cruchley, London.

Davis, R., 2012, *A Concise History of Western Australia*. Woodslane Press, Sydney.

Delgardo, A., 1971, *A Victorian Entertainment*. American Heritage Press, New York.

Dinham, M., Personal correspondence.

Dinham, M., 1997, *Travels to Exotic Places*. Self published.

Dutton, G., 1984, *Founder of a City: The Life of Colonel William Light*. Rigby, Adelaide.

Estensen, M., 2003, *Matthew Flinders*. Allen and Unwin, Sydney.

Fitzhardinge, L.F., 1973, *Old Canberra and the Search for a Capital*. Canberra Historical Society, Canberra.

Fuss, E., Private correspondence. Burra History Group.

Gale, J., 1907, *The federal capital, Dalgety or Canberra, which?: a paper*. Queanbeyan, NSW.

Gaston, A., 1984, *Coolgardie Gold—Personal Record*. Hesperian Press, Perth.

Gemmell, N., 1995, *Old Strathalbyn and its People*. National Trust of South Australia, Adelaide.

Goulburn Heritage Group, 2010, *EC Manfred—Goulburn Architect and Surveyor: A Glimpse of his Works 1880–1892*. Exhibition at Goulburn Regional Art Gallery.

Gray, F., (Archivist of the Northern Agricultural Association Singleton), Personal correspondence.

Gunn, A., 1987, *We of the Never Never*. Angus and Robertson, Sydney.

Heritage Citation Report, 2013, Stonnington History Centre.

Heritage South Australia website.

Heydon, P., 1987, *Just a Century Ago—A History of the Shire of Cue*. Hesperian Press, Perth.

Heydon, P., 2008, *Gold on the Murchison*. Hesperian Press, Perth.

Historic Places, 1982, Heritage Reprints, pp. 192–201. Australian Council of National Trusts, Canberra.

Hughes, R., 1987, *The Fatal Shore—A History of the Transportation of Convicts to Australia 1787–1868*. Collins Harvill, London.

Hunter, C., 1996, *West Maitland Park—A History*. Maitland City Council.

James, G. and Lee, C., 1975, *Walhalla Heyday*. Reprint by Graham Publications, Ringwood, Victoria.

Johnstone Park Draft Conservation Management Plan.

Jones, D., 1999, *Strathalbyn Soldiers' Memorial Gardens Conservation and Management Study*. Alexandrina Council and Heritage SA.

Keesing, N. (ed), 1971, *History of the Australian Gold Rushes—By Those Who Were There*. Lloyd O'Neil, Hawthorn, Victoria.

Kerr, M. and C., 1975, *The River Men*. Rigby, Adelaide.

Knox, M., 2013, *Boom—The Underground History of Australia from Gold Rush to GFC*. Penguin/Viking, Melbourne.

Launceston City Council. Launceston's Cataract Gorge Reserve brochure.

Launceston Examiner newspaper, 8 September 1907.

Lovekin, A., 1925, *The King's Park, Perth*. E.S. Wigg and Co., Perth.

Lund, in Tanner, H. (ed) 1981, *Architects of Australia*. Macmillan, Melbourne.

Macfarlane's Cast Iron Catalogues. Saracen Foundry, Glasgow.

Maitland, B., 1999, *The Pender Index: A Guide to the Architectural Work of the Pender Practice of Maitland NSW 1863–1988*. University of Newcastle, Newcastle.

Mannum Dock Museum of River History website.

Marquis-Kyle, P. and Walker, M., 1996, *The Illustrated Burra Charter*. Australian Heritage Commission, Canberra.

Maslin, T.J., 1830, *The Friend of Australia; or, a Plan for Exploring the Interior, and for Carrying on a Survey of the Whole Continent of Australia*. By a Retired Officer of the Hon. East India Company's Service. Hurst, Chance, and Co., London.

Maxwell, M., 1959, *Written in Gold*. The Mudgee Newspaper, Mudgee.

McClymont, J., 2001, *Pictorial History Parramatta District*. Kingsclear Books, Sydney.

Melbourne City Council, Parks and Gardens Division, 1984, *Melbourne Parks and Gardens History, Features and Statistics*.

Menghettie, D., 1984, *Charters Towers*. PhD thesis, James Cook University, Townsville.

Monument Australia website.

Morris, E.E. (ed.), 1980, *Australia's First Century 1788–1888*. Child and Henry, Hornsby.

National Trust of Australia (NSW), 1996, *Showgrounds of NSW Study*. Sydney.

Patrick, J., 2008, *Fitzroy Gardens Conservation Management Plan*.

Pattie, R., 2000, *History of the City of Ballarat Municipal Brass Band—100 Years of Music to the Citizens of Ballarat*. ballaratbrassband.com.au.

Paull, R., 2003, *Old Walhalla—Portrait of a Gippsland Gold Town*. Revised by Paoletti, R. Paoletti's Maps and Videos P/L, Langwarrin, Victoria.

Peach, W., 1976, *Peach's Australia*. Australian Broadcasting Commission, Sydney.

Pegrum, R., 2008, *The Bush Capital*. Watermark Press, Boorowa. Second edition.

Penalver, D., (undated), *A Self-guided Walking Tour around Goulburn's Church Hill Featuring the Architecture of EC Manfred, a Great Victorian Architect*. Hypercet, Goulburn.

Penalver, D., 2012, *Self-guided Walking Tour of Goulburn's West End Featuring the Architecture of EC Manfred, a Great Victorian Architect*. Hypercet, Goulburn.

Penalver, D., Penalver, P. and Cooper, L., 2013, *EC Manfred—Architect and Surveyor, Goulburn*. Hypercet, Goulburn.

Plant Location International Feasibility Study, 2 September 1971.

Pollon, F., 1983, *Parramatta the Cradle City of Australia*. The Council of the City of Parramatta.

Prahran Council Minutes. 1885, 1890, 1891, 1894, 1895. (No minutes are extant for 1892, 1893.)

Pyrenees Advocate, April 1903, 12 March 2004.

Queen of the Murchison—A Visitors Guide to the Cue District. Presented by the Cue Pre-School 1976. Cue Shire Council.

Reader's Digest Book of Historic Australian Towns, 1982. Reader's Digest Services Pty Ltd.

Reedman, L., 2008, *Early Architects of the Hunter Region—A Hundred Years to 1940*. Les Reedman and Margaret Walker.

Rees, L., 1980, Letter to Lane Cove Council, 12 March.

Register of New South Wales War Memorials website.

Register of the National Estate—Heritage database.

Reynolds, H., 2012, *A History of Tasmania*. Cambridge University Press, Cambridge.

Reynolds, J., 1969, *Launceston: History of an Australian City*. Macmillan, Melbourne.

Riponshire Advocate, May, September, December 1903.

Robertson, E.G., 1977, *Cast Iron Decoration—A World Survey*. Thames and Hudson, Melbourne.

Roderick, D., 1984, *The Town they Called "the World"*. Boolarong Publications.

Russell, E., 1970, *A North Shore History, Lane Cove—1788, 1895, 1970*. The Council of the Municipality of Lane Cove.

Russell, E., 1995, *A Century of Change—Lane Cove Municipality 1895–1995*. The Council of the Municipality of Lane Cove.

Shakespeare, N., 2006, *In Tasmania*. Random House Australia.

Singleton Historical Society and Museum, 2011, *Singleton Buildings Then and Now*. Singleton.

Stannage, C., 1979, *The People of Perth—A Social History of Western Australia's Capital City*. Perth City Council, Perth.

Statham, J., 2012, *Heritage Study no. 60597*.

Stephenson, P., 1966, *The History and Description of Sydney Harbour*. Rigby, Adelaide.

Stevenson, Kay, 2014, Personal correspondence.

Strudwick, S., 2012, *The Murray River—One River, Many Lands*. Australian Broadcasting Commission, Sydney.

Strugnell, R., Personal correspondence.

Stuart, D., 1988, *The Garden Triumphant—A Victorian Legacy*. Harper and Rowe, New York.

Tazewell, S., 1991, *Grand Goulburn, First Inland City of Australia: A Random History*. Council of the City of Goulburn.

Tench, W., 1789, *1788*, T. Flannery (ed.), 2000. Text Publishing, Melbourne.

The Mercury newspaper, 22 December 1925.

The West Australian newspaper, 24 September 1904.

Timms, P., 2010, *In Search of Hobart*. New South Publishing, Sydney.

Townsville Library Local History Special Collections—Townsville Council Minutes.

Trollope, A., 1873, *Australia*, Edwards, P. and Joyce, R. (eds.), 1967. University of Queensland Press, Brisbane.

Trollope, A., 1966, *Trollope's Australia*, H. Dow (ed.). Thomas Nelson, Melbourne and Sydney.

Twain, M., *The Wayward Tourist—Mark Twain's Adventures in Australia—introduced by Don Watson*. Melbourne University Press, Melbourne, 2006 edition.

Victorian Heritage Register.

Videon, T., 1988, *And the Band Played On ... Band Rotundas of Victoria*. MA thesis, Monash University.

Wannan, W., 1978, *Riverboat—Stories of Old Australia*. Sun Books, Melbourne.

Watson, A. (ed.), 1998, *Beyond Architecture—Marion Mahony and Walter Burley Griffin—America, Australia, India*. Powerhouse Publishing, Sydney.

West, P., 1990, *A History of Parramatta*. Kangaroo Press, Sydney.

Whitehead, G., 1997, *Civilising the City—A History of Melbourne's Public Gardens*. State Library of Victoria, Melbourne.

Whitehead, G., Talk on Clement Hodgkinson to Collingwood Historical Society, 25 August 2009.

Wild, S., 1993, *The History of Prahran Vol II 1925–1990*. Melbourne University Press, Melbourne.

Wright, R., 1989, *The Bureaucrat's Domain*. Oxford University Press, Oxford.

Wyatt, T., 1995, *The History of Goulburn, NSW*. Municipality of Goulburn.

photo credits

Photography is by Belinda Brown, unless otherwise credited.
http://www.belindabrownphotography.co.nz/

Introduction

p4–5 Carol service at Central Park, Armidale. Courtesy Eric Grigg.
p6 Mughal Pavilion. Crowe, *The Gardens of Mughul India*, Thames and Hudson, London.
Temple of Music, West Wycombe Park. Wikimedia Commons.
The Dancing Platform at Cremorne Gardens. *Illustrated London News*, June 1851.
p8 The Royal Horticultural Bandstand, Kensington. Bradbury, M., *Pavilion for Music*, p.12.
p9 Miners' Aggregate Meeting, Lambton Park, Newcastle. Courtesy University of Newcastle Cultural Collections.
p13 S.T. Gill., 'Off to the Diggings. Sketches of the Victorian Gold Diggings etc. 1852–53'. Courtesy Dixon Library, State Library of New South Wales.

p14 Poster for Cremorne Gardens, Sydney. Stanton Library local collection.
p16 Arriving by ferry at Correy's Pleasure Garden. Courtesy Canada Bay Library Service.
p17 Glebe Wireless House. Photo by author.

Queensland

Townsville, p32 Opening of Bandstand on the Strand. North Queensland Photographic Collection, James Cook University, Special Collections.

New South Wales

Lane Cove, p42–43 Pavilion photos by author.
Lane Cove, p42 Sculpture of Lloyd Rees by Lawrence Beck. Courtesy Sydney City Council.
Gulgong, p46 Street scene, Gulgong c1870–75. Holterman Collection. Courtesy Mitchell Library, State Library of New South Wales.

Singleton, p60–64 Photos by author.
Singleton, p62 Photo of Singleton Town Band, 1929. Courtesy Singleton Town Band.

Victoria

Fitzroy Gardens, p70 The Kiosk, c1910. Courtesy Fitzroy Gardens, City of Melbourne Parks and Gardens.

South Australia

Market Square, p114 The Ladies' Cheer Up Band with the Navy, Navy Day 1917. Courtesy The Burra History Group Inc.

Western Australia

Cue, p132 Dr Ramsey's Hospital Tent, Cue 1895. Courtesy State Library of Western Australia.

Northern Territory

Katherine, p134 Photo by Warwick Lidgard.

acknowledgements

United Kingdom
Ali Davey, Historic Scotland

New Zealand
Warwick Lidgard

Queensland
Dr Valerie Dennis, National Trust, Queensland
Steven Pritchard, Mackay Historical Society
Barbara Mathieson, Townsville Library
Colleen Moss, Charters Towers Excelsior Library
Janice Dowman, Maryborough

New South Wales
Jill Bennett, Newcastle Region Library
Judy Nichols, Maitland Library
Bronwyn Hanna
Amanda Keevil, Ashfield Library
Shayne Bray, Parramatta Heritage Centre
Linda Cooper, Goulburn
Peter FitzSimons, Sydney
Natalie Dimmock, Singleton Library

Amanda Crnkovic, Liverpool City Band
Cathie Lamont, Armidale City Band
Roslyn Maddrel, Braidwood Library
Naomi Bassford, Lane Cove Library
Barry Maitland
Philip Playford

Australian Capital Territory
Peter Freeman & Partners

Victoria
Tracey Videon, author of *The Band Played On*
  Thesis on Bandstands and Rotundas in Victoria
Sue-Ann Williams, Lovell Chen, Melbourne
Jill and Trevor Riches, Strathalbyn
Martin Turner and Bryce Rayworth, Melbourne
Shirley Boyle, Beaufort Historical Society
John Statham, Lovell Chen, Melbourne
Professor Miles Lewis, Fitzroy, Melbourne
Ellen Porter, Storrington History Centre (special thanks)
Robert Strugnell, Fitzroy Gardens, Melbourne

Tasmania
Catherine Pearce, State Library
Geraldine Morehead

South Australia
Eric Fuss and Meredith Satchell, Burra History Group
Kay Stevenson, Mannum
Bob Dodd, Wallaroo Museum

Western Australia
Ruth Lee, Cue Community Resource Centre
Karen Morrisey and Mollie Dinham
Timothy Moore, Local History Centre, Kalgoorlie
Tess Thomson, Eastern Goldfields Historical Society, Boulder
Sue Smith and Jenny Reid, Albany Public Library
Dr John Taylor, Architect, Perth

Northern Territory
Kerryn Taylor, Kay Marsh and Simone Croft, Katherine Museum